Editor
Erica N. Russikoff, M.A.

Editor in Chief
Karen J. Goldfluss, M.S. Ed.

Cover Artist
Tony Carrillo
Brenda DiAntonis

Imaging
James Edward Grace

Publisher
Mary D. Smith, M.S. Ed.

Teacher Created Resources
TCR 5031

DAILY WARM-UPS
Nonfiction Reading — Grade 1

Includes:

- 150 leveled passages with a variety of interesting topics
- Comprehension questions that target reading skills & strategies
- Standards & Benchmarks

Ideal for test preparation

30 passages & activities in each of these sections:
Interesting Places & Events
Scientifically Speaking
From the Past
Did You Know?
Fascinating People

Teacher Created Resources

Author
Ruth Foster, M. Ed.

Teacher Created Resources
6421 Industry Way
Westminster, CA 92683
www.teachercreated.com
ISBN: 978-1-4206-5031-0
© 2011 Teacher Created Resources
Made in U.S.A.

Teacher Created Resources

Table of Contents

Introduction 4

Standards and Benchmarks 6

Interesting Places and Events 7

   Raining Fish 9

   The Black Cloud 10

   A City Without Cars 11

   Should You Wear a Raincoat? 12

   A Kangaroo Hero 13

   Nodding "No" 14

   The Window Washer 15

   Getting Ready for Antarctica 16

   The Only Place 17

   A Salt Mine 18

   The Biggest Antique Ever Sold 19

   Mail on Stilts 20

   Easter Island 21

   Getting to the Top 22

   A Diamond to Keep 23

   A Big Food Fight 24

   A Wet Side and a Dry Side 25

   The Biggest Country 26

   A State That Grows 27

   A Strange Find 28

   What They Race in Qatar 29

   Airport Island 30

   Too Wet for a Race 31

   A Name That Was a Trick 32

   A Bridge to Jump Off 33

   Idaho Before the Moon 34

   A Gray Suit 35

   A Famous Tower 36

   A House on Stilts 37

   Day and Night Are the Same 38

Scientifically Speaking 39

   The Most Bones 41

   The Turtle's Tears 42

   Clam Drop 43

   The Longest and the Shortest Days 44

   The Hungry Shark 45

   The First Refrigerator 46

   A True Super Suit 47

   A Snake That Can Catch a Bat 48

   What the Owl Throws Up 49

   Why Astronauts Sneeze 50

   Popcorn 51

   Why Spiders Don't Get Stuck 52

   The Most Kinds 53

   The Quiet Flyer 54

   Different Seasons 55

   The Place to Throw Far 56

   Plant Trap 57

   What the Rings Tell 58

   Impossible to Sink 59

   How to Tell the Oldest Mountains 60

   Twinkling Stars 61

   Dinosaur Fossils 62

   Claws of the Fastest 63

   The Darker Hand 64

   Blue Blood 65

   Wolf Den 66

   Doctors Who Spread Germs 67

   Why We Burp 68

   Make It Go One Hundred Miles an Hour! . . . 69

   A Horse That Bolted 70

From the Past 71

   An Old Hairstyle 73

   Cleaning Without Soap 74

   A Game with a Snake 75

   Birthday Count 76

   May You Sit? 77

   The Moat 78

   The Hammock 79

   Left Foot, Right Foot 80

   How Many Knots? 81

   Rescue Dogs 82

   Wearing a Cage 83

   Why the Tree Was Scraped 84

   Talking with Signs 85

   Gifts for the Guests 86

   Sodbusters 87

   The First Rubber Ball 88

Table of Contents (cont.)

How to Be Polite in a Tepee 89
How to Pack 90
Did Kids Drink Milk? 91
Fishing with Birds 92
Easier Not to Smile 93
A High-Priced Meal 94
Toothbrushes 95
A Land of Invention 96
Why People Burned Bamboo 97
Fuel on the Plains 98
Pitch Lake 99
A Secret 100
Pigeon Heroes 101
The Bad Wish 102

Did You Know? 103
Can You Run Faster Than a Flying Bird? . . .105
You and the Rhino 106
Seventeen Years Underground 107
From Ship to Building 108
Don't Open the Window! 109
A Fruit That Can't Go on a Train 110
Why People Wore Antlers on Their Eyes . . .111
Most Buildings Are Made Of . . .? 112
Why Beekeepers Work at Night 113
Silly Laws .114
A Flower That Stinks 115
Hurricane Names 116
The Fox and the Badger 117
Tail Talking 118
Climbing a Waterfall 119
The Song Most Sung 120
Wet Money 121
Baby Eyes That Look Big 122
Charming Cobras 123
Word in Reverse 124
The Fishing Cat 125
Blue from Space 126
In the Mouth of a Crocodile 127
All About Antlers 128
Ouch! 129
Ants for Stitching 130

First in the Air 131
Scurvy 132
What the Otter Uses 133
The Baby's Ride 134

Fascinating People 135
Tightrope Walker 137
The Sailor Without Shoes 138
What Frank Forgot 139
Swimming Through Hot and Cold 140
Walking to a Lesson 141
Nonstop Around the World 142
The Alaskan Flag 143
Gorilla Lady 144
The Mad Cook 145
Short Lessons 146
How Gino Zoomed 147
From No-Good to Good 148
A Dog and Flares 149
Something New at the White House 150
Dancing on Ice 151
A Lost President 152
Losing Eighty Times 153
Pen Name .154
Why the Hedges Were Trimmed 155
What Ben Didn't Do 156
The Old Lady That Wasn't 157
Swimming at the Poles 158
No One Knew 159
What Saved Susan 160
A Twisted Wire 161
A Sleeping Bag with Hooks 162
Pushing Wheels 163
A Polite Traveler 164
Sixteen Sunrises 165
Air Stunt 166

Answer Key 167

Leveling Chart 174

Tracking Sheet 175

Award Certificate 176

Introduction

The primary goal of any reading task is comprehension. *Daily Warm-Ups: Nonfiction Reading* uses high-interest, grade-level appropriate nonfiction passages followed by assessment practice to help develop confident readers who can demonstrate their skills on standardized tests. Each passage is a high-interest nonfiction text that fits one of the five topic areas: Interesting Places and Events, Scientifically Speaking, From the Past, Did You Know?, and Fascinating People. Each of these five topic areas has 30 passages, for a total of 150 passages. Each passage, as well as its corresponding multiple-choice assessment questions, is provided on one page.

Comprehension Questions

The questions in *Daily Warm-Ups: Nonfiction Reading* assess all levels of comprehension, from basic recall to critical thinking. The questions are based on fundamental reading skills found in scope-and-sequence charts across the nation:

- recall information
- use prior knowledge
- visualize
- recognize the main idea
- identify supporting details
- understand cause and effect

- sequence in chronological order
- identify synonyms and antonyms
- know grade-level vocabulary
- use context clues to understand new words
- make inferences
- draw conclusions

Readability

The texts have a 0.0–2.0 grade level based on the Flesch-Kincaid Readability Formula. This formula, built into Microsoft Word®, determines readability by calculating the number of words, syllables, and sentences. Multisyllabic words tend to skew the grade level, making it appear higher than it actually is. Refer to the Leveling Chart on page 174 for the approximate grade level of each passage.

Including Standards and Benchmarks

The passages and comprehension questions throughout this book correlate with McREL (Mid-Continent Research for Education and Learning) Standards. Known as a "Compendium of Standards and Benchmarks," this resource is well researched. It includes standards and benchmarks that represent a consolidation of national and state standards in several content areas for grades K–12. (See page 6 for the specific McREL Standards and Benchmarks that correspond with this book.) These standards can be aligned to the Common Core Standards. To do so, please visit *www.mcrel.org*.

Practice First to Build Familiarity

Initial group practice is essential. Read aloud the first passage in each of the five topic areas and do its related questions with the whole class. Depending upon the needs of your class, you may choose to do the first three passages in each topic area as a whole class. Some teachers like to use five days in a row to model the reading and question-answering process at the start of the year. Model pre-reading the questions, reading the text, highlighting information that refers to the comprehension questions, and eliminating answers that are obviously incorrect. You may also want to model referring back to the text to ensure the answers selected are the best ones.

Introduction (cont.)

Student Practice Ideas

With *Daily Warm-Ups: Nonfiction Reading* you can choose to do whole-class or independent practice. For example, you can use the passages and questions for the following:

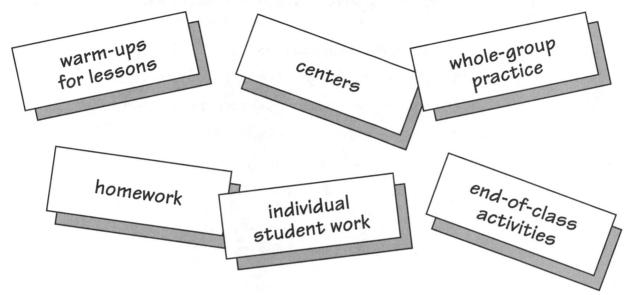

warm-ups for lessons

centers

whole-group practice

homework

individual student work

end-of-class activities

Whichever method you choose for using the book, it's a good idea to practice as a class how to read a passage and respond to the comprehension questions. In this way, you can demonstrate your own thought processes by "thinking aloud" to figure out an answer. Essentially, this means that you tell your students your thoughts as they come to you.

Record Keeping

In the sun image at the bottom, right-hand corner of each warm-up page, there is a place for you (or for students) to write the number of questions answered correctly. This will give consistency to scored pages. Use the Tracking Sheet on page 175 to record which warm-up exercises you have given to your students. Or distribute copies of the sheet for students to keep their own records. Use the certificate on page 176 as you see fit; for example, you can use the certificate as a reward for students who complete a certain amount of warm-up exercises.

How to Make the Most of This Book

- ✏ Read each lesson ahead of time before you use it with the class so that you are familiar with it. This will make it easier to answer students' questions.

- ✏ Set aside ten to twelve minutes at a specific time daily to incorporate *Daily Warm-Ups: Nonfiction Reading* into your routine.

- ✏ Make sure the time you spend working on the materials is positive and constructive. This should be a time of practicing for success and recognizing it as it is achieved.

The passages and comprehension questions in *Daily Warm-Ups: Nonfiction Reading* are time-efficient, allowing your students to practice these skills often. The more your students practice reading and responding to content-area comprehension questions, the more confident and competent they will become.

Standards and Benchmarks

Each passage in *Daily Warm-Ups: Nonfiction Reading* meets at least one of the following standards and benchmarks, which are used with permission from McREL. Copyright 2010 McREL. Mid-continent Research for Education and Learning. 4601 DTC Boulevard, Suite 500, Denver, CO 80237. Telephone: 303-337-0990. Web site: *www.mcrel.org/standards-benchmarks*. To align McREL Standards to the Common Core Standards, go to *www.mcrel.org*.

Uses the general skills and strategies of the reading process

- Uses mental images based on pictures and print to aid in comprehension of text
- Uses meaning clues to aid comprehension and make predictions about content
- Uses basic elements of phonetic analysis to decode unknown words
- Uses basic elements of structural analysis to decode unknown words
- Understands level-appropriate sight words and vocabulary
- Uses self-correction strategies

Uses skills and strategies to read a variety of informational texts

- Reads a variety of informational texts
- Understands the main idea and supporting details of simple expository information
- Relates new information to prior knowledge and experience

Uses meaning clues to aid comprehension and make predictions about content

Understands the main idea and supporting details of simple expository information

Interesting Places and Events

Warm-Up

1

Name _____

Raining Fish

Great Yarmouth is a town. It is in England. It is a **port town**. A port town has a place where ships can load and unload. A strange thing happened in this town. It happened on August 6, 2000. What happened? It rained fish!

A tornado is a wind. It forms a cloud. The cloud spins. A small tornado at sea picked up seawater as it spun. Fish got picked up, too. The cloud moved over the town. Fish rained down from the cloud!

Find the Answers

1. A **port town** must be

    a. close to rocks.

    b. close to water.

    c. close to a desert.

    d. close to mountains.

2. It rained fish on

    a. August 6, 2000.

    b. August 9, 2000.

    c. August 9, 2006.

    d. August 6, 2009.

3. Most likely, when it rained fish, people were

    a. hot.

    b. sleepy.

    c. reading.

    d. surprised.

/3

Warm-Up 2

Name _____

The Black Cloud

Jim White was a cowboy. In 1901, he saw a strange, black cloud. The cloud seemed to come out of the ground. Jim watched the cloud. He saw that it was not a cloud. It was millions of bats.

Jim went exploring. He wanted to find out where the bats were coming from. They were coming out of a hole. Jim took a lantern and a rope. He went down the dark hole. He went deep underground.

 What did Jim find? He found a huge cave. It was filled with passageways and large rooms. Bats slept in the cave during the day. Today, the cave is a park. It is called Carlsbad Caverns. It is in New Mexico.

Find the Answers

1. The strange, black cloud was
   a. a dark hole.
   b. a passageway.
   c. millions of bats.
   d. deep underground.

2. Where is the cave Jim found?
   a. Bee Mexico
   b. Far Mexico
   c. Old Mexico
   d. New Mexico

3. Most likely, Jim saw the cloud near
   a. the end of the day.
   b. the start of the day.
   c. the middle of the day.
   d. the middle of the night.

 /3

Warm-Up
3

Name _____

A City Without Cars

Venice is a city in Italy. It is an old city. It is very beautiful. You want to explore Venice. You want to see its beautiful buildings. Do you take a car? Do you take a bus? Do you take an airplane?

You can't take a car. You can't take a bus. You can't take an airplane. They are not allowed!

How do people get around? How do they explore the city? They take boats! Venice is filled with canals. The canals go up and down. The canals are like streets.

Find the Answers

1. What is *not* true about Venice?

    a. It is old.   c. It allows cars.

    b. It has canals.   d. It is in Italy.

2. From the story, you can tell that the canals must be filled with

    a. dirt.   c. water.

    b. sand.   d. roads.

3. If you go to see new things, you

    a. sing.   c. sleep.

    b. exit.   d. explore.

/3

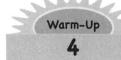

Warm-Up
4

Name _____

Should You Wear a Raincoat?

You live in Hawaii. You live on Mt. Waialeale. You go outside. Should you bring a raincoat?

You live in Chile. You live in the Atacama Desert. You go outside. Should you bring a raincoat?

A year has 365 days. On Mt. Waialeale, it can rain a lot. It can rain 350 days of the year. It rains nearly every day of the year. Yes, you should bring a raincoat!

The Atacama Desert is very dry. It is the driest place in the world. It rarely rains. Less than .04 inches of rain falls in a year. You do not need a raincoat!

Find the Answers

1. Where is Mt. Waialeale?
  a. Chile   c. Canada
  b. Hawaii   d. Hungary

2. Most likely, if you didn't bring a raincoat on Mt. Waialeale, you would get
  a. wet.   c. hungry.
  b. hot.   d. sleepy.

3. If something doesn't happen very often, it is
  a. dry.   c. rare.
  b. near.   d. outside.

/3

Name _____

Warm-Up 5

A Kangaroo Hero

Lulu is a kangaroo. Her mother was hit by a car.
She was **rescued** by a farmer. The farmer lived in
Australia. His name was Len Richards. Len took
good care of Lulu.

There was a big storm. A big branch fell out of a tree. It hit Len on the
head. It knocked him out. Lulu knew Len needed help. She knew he was
badly hurt. She knew she needed to get him help.

Lulu barked. She barked and barked. She did not stop until someone
helped Len. A farmer rescued a kangaroo. Then the kangaroo rescued a
farmer! Lulu was given an award for being a hero.

Find the Answers

1. When something is **rescued**, it is
   a. knocked out.   c. given an award.
   b. lost or hurt.   d. saved or helped.

2. Where does Lulu live?
   a. Asia   c. North America
   b. Australia   d. South America

3. If someone did *not* read the whole story, he or she might think Lulu was a
   a. dog because she barked.   c. cow because she barked.
   b. cat because she barked.   d. horse because she barked.

/3

Warm-Up

6

Name _____

Nodding "No"

How do you say "yes" without words? How do you say "no" without words? To say "yes," you nod your head. You nod it up and down. To say "no," you shake your head. You shake it side to side.

Watch out! If you go to Sri Lanka or Bulgaria, it is not the same. In these two countries, you do not nod your head up and down to say "yes." You shake it side to side! You do not shake your head side to side to say "no." You nod it up and down!

Find the Answers

1. If people from Bulgaria wanted to say "no," they would

    a. shake your hand.

    b. smile and turn around.

    c. nod their heads up and down.

    d. shake their heads from side to side.

2. Why might you want to know what other people do in other countries?

    a. You want to be rude.

    b. You want to be polite.

    c. You want to make a mistake.

    d. You want to make people angry.

3. Nodding your head up and down

    a. never means "no."

    b. always means "no."

    c. always means "yes."

    d. sometimes means "no."

/3

Name _____

**Warm-Up
7**

The Window Washer

The Louvre is a museum. It is in France. It is filled with art. It is one of the largest museums in the world. It has two pyramids. The pyramids have four sides. The sides are triangles. The sides are made of glass.

How are the pyramids cleaned? The sides are very tall. The sides cannot be climbed. They would break.

A robot cleans the glass! The robot goes up the glass sides. It goes across the glass. It goes down the glass. It is not too heavy. Its weight does not break the glass. How does the window–washing robot stay on? It stays on by suction.

Find the Answers

1. How many sides do these pyramids have?

a. one   c. four

b. three   d. five

2. From the story, you can tell that the robot

a. weighs less than a person.   c. weighs more than the pyramids.

b. weighs more than a person.   d. weighs about the same as a person.

3. Most likely, when a fly walks up a wall, it stays on by

a. washing.   c. holding.

b. suction.   d. cleaning.

/3

Name _____

Warm-Up 8

Getting Ready for Antarctica

A marathon is a race. Runners race far. They run 26.2 miles. One marathon was in Antarctica. Antarctica is very cold. There are strong winds. There is ice and snow.

One runner lived where it was hot. How was he going to get ready for the race? How could he get ready for the cold, wind, ice, and snow?

The man ran in a freezer! The freezer was big. Ice cream was stored there. He rode a bike in the freezer, too. The bike stayed in one place. He put a big, strong fan by the bike. When he biked, the fan blew cold air on him.

Find the Answers

1. What would the man most likely say?

a. Running a marathon is easy.

b. You must get ready before running a marathon.

c. Running a marathon in the hot and cold is the same.

d. You only need to run to get ready for a marathon.

2. When the man turned the fan on, he was getting ready for the Antarctic

a. ice.   c. wind.

b. cold.   d. snow.

3. What was stored in the freezer?

a. meat   c. apples

b. juice   d. ice cream

/3

Warm-Up
9

Name _____

The Only Place

The sun rises in the east. The sun **sets** in the west. There is only one place in the world where you can see something special. What can you see? You can see the sun rise and set over two oceans.

Panama is a country. It is not very wide. You can stand on a hill. Look to the east. You can see the Atlantic Ocean. Look to the west. You can see the Pacific Ocean.

In the morning, you can see the sun rise. In the evening, you can see the sun set. The sun rises over the Atlantic. It sets over the Pacific. You cannot see this anywhere else.

Find the Answers

1. You can only see the sun rise and set over two oceans because Panama is *not* very

    a. tiny.   c. wide.

    b. cold.   d. small.

2. What word means the opposite of **set**?

    a. run   c. skip

    b. rise   d. sleep

3. Where does the sun rise where you live?

    a. east   c. north

    b. west   d. south

/3

Warm-Up
10

Name _____

A Salt Mine

A very old mine is in Poland. What is **mined**? What is taken out of the ground? Salt is mined. Salt has been taken out of the ground for hundreds of years.

The mine is very big. It has several levels. Inside, miners have carved out big rooms. They have carved out statues. They have carved out benches. They have carved out a church. They have carved out all these things from salt.

If you want, you can rent a room in the mine. You can have a big party under the ground in a room carved out of salt!

Find the Answers

1. When something is **mined**, it is
    a. washed off hands.
    b. read from books.
    c. carved out of salt.
    d. taken out of the ground.

2. The story does *not* tell you
    a. what the statues look like.
    b. who carved out the statues.
    c. what the statues are made of.
    d. what country the statues are in.

3. Salt has been mined from the mine for
    a. hundreds of days.
    b. hundreds of years.
    c. hundreds of hours.
    d. hundreds of weeks.

/3

Warm-Up 11

Name _____

The Biggest Antique Ever Sold

What is an **antique**? An antique is something very old. It could be a book or a dish. It could be a tool.

People sell antiques. One man bought an antique. It was the biggest antique ever sold. What was the antique? It was a bridge!

The bridge was London Bridge. It was built in London. London is in England. It was used in 1831. It had five arches. It was made of stones. The bridge was moved when it was sold. It was taken to Arizona. Arizona is in the United States. The old stones were used in a new bridge.

Find the Answers

1. What is *not* true about the bridge?

   a. It had six arches.

   b. It was made of stones.

   c. It was built in London.

   d. It was taken to Arizona.

2. Most likely, the bridge

   a. was not an antique.

   b. was used long before 1831.

   c. was rebuilt with new stones.

   d. was taken apart before it was moved.

3. What might be an **antique**?

   a. a new house

   b. your pet cat

   c. your grandmother's doll

   d. an apple you ate for lunch

/3

Warm-Up

12   Name _____

Mail on Stilts

The mail arrives. Did your mail person bring it on foot? Did he or she bring it by truck? France is a country. In one part of France, the mail once came a different way. Postmen wore stilts! The stilts were high. They made the postmen very tall.

Why did the postmen wear stilts? There was a lot of underbrush. There were lots of brambles. There were lots of **marshy** areas. The postmen did not want to get scratched. They did not want to get wet. Up high, they were away from the brambles. They were dry.

The postmen could take big steps. They could go fast. The postmen carried long poles. The long poles helped them keep their balance.

Find the Answers

1. From the story, you can tell that a **marshy** area is

   a. hot.   c. wet.

   b. dry.   d. high.

2. What helped a postman keep his balance?

   a. a bag   c. a rope

   b. a pole   d. a letter

3. Most likely, mail people don't use stilts today because

   a. there are cleared roads.   c. there are roads with underbrush.

   b. they lost their long poles.   d. they got scratched by the brambles.

/3

Name _____

Warm-Up
13

Easter Island

Easter Island is very small. It is in the Pacific Ocean. It is far away from other lands. It is very hard to get to. It has little water. Very few people live there.

Statues dot the island. The statues are big heads. They are made of stone. They are old. There are a lot of them. There are about eight hundred.

The island has something else on it. It is very long. There is only one. It is not as old. What is it? It is a runway. It is for a space shuttle. It is for an **emergency** landing.

Find the Answers

1. About how many stone heads are there?

   a. one

   b. eighty

   c. one hundred

   d. eight hundred

2. What is *not* a reason why very few people live on Easter Island?

   a. It is very small.

   b. It has little water.

   c. It has a long runway.

   d. It is very hard to get to.

3. If there is an **emergency**, something

   a. needs to be done right away.

   b. needs to be done over a long time.

   c. needs to be done in water.

   d. needs to be done to the stone heads.

/3

Warm-Up 14

Name _____

Getting to the Top

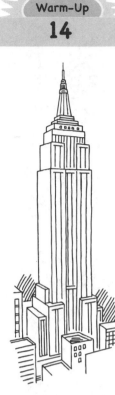

The Empire State Building is tall. It is in New York. It opened in 1931. It was the tallest building in the world for forty years. Then taller buildings were built.

Many people come to see it. They ride elevators to go to the top. They look out over the city. How long is the ride to the top? It is not **long**. It is short. It takes about a minute.

One day each year people do not ride. They do not use the elevators. What do they do? They race! They race up the stairs. They climb 1,576 stairs! One man went very fast. He reached the top in less then ten minutes!

Find the Answers

1. The opposite of **long** is

a. fast.   c. short.

b. tall.   d. reach.

2. How many times is the race held each year?

a. 1   c. 40

b. 10   d. 1,576

3. How do most people get to the top of the Empire State Building?

a. They climb the walls.   c. They walk up the stairs.

b. They race up the stairs.   d. They ride in elevators.

/3

Name _____

Warm-Up 15

A Diamond to Keep

You can go to a diamond mine. The mine is in Arkansas. It is a state park. The park is called Crater of Diamonds State Park. You can do something at the park. You can dig for **diamonds**!

What if you find a diamond? Do you have to give it back? No, you can keep it! You can keep every gem you find. Two or three diamonds are found each day. Most diamonds are small. Some diamonds are big. The big diamonds are worth a lot of money.

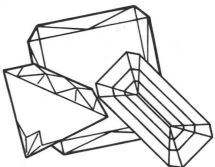

Find the Answers

1. A **diamond** is a kind of

a. gem.   c. state.

b. park.   d. crater.

2. What state is the diamond mine in?

a. Alaska   c. Arizona

b. Alabama   d. Arkansas

3. If you find a diamond at this park,

a. it is small.   c. it is something you can keep.

b. it is worth a lot of money.   d. it is something you have to give back.

/3

Warm-Up

16

Name _____

A Big Food Fight

Once a year, something special happens in Spain. It is in a small town in Spain. It happens in a small town, but it is something big. What is it? It is the biggest food fight in the world!

People throw tomatoes. The tomatoes are brought in by the truckload. The tomatoes are not for eating. They are just for throwing. They are dumped onto the street. When it is time, people pick up the tomatoes. They throw them at each other. They have a good time making a big mess.

Find the Answers

1. Most likely, what happens right after the food fight?

   a. People clean up the big mess.

   b. People dump more tomatoes onto the street.

   c. People have another food fight the next day.

   d. People eat all the tomatoes that were thrown.

2. What words from the story let you know that there are a lot of tomatoes?

   a. "not for eating"   c. "brought in by the truckload"

   b. "dumped onto the street"   d. "good time making a big mess"

3. Where does the fight take place?

   a. a big town in Spain   c. a big town in Tanzania

   b. a small town in Spain   d. a small town in Tanzania

/3

Name _____

Warm-Up
17   **A Wet Side and a Dry Side**

Washington is a state. It has a wet side. It has a dry side. Why is it so wet on one side of the state? Why is it so dry on the other?

Winds blow. They blow west to east. The winds push rain clouds. Something stops the rain clouds. Mountains stop the rain clouds. The mountains are called the Cascades. The rain clouds can't get past the Cascades' high **peaks.**

The rain clouds stay on the west side of the mountains. They stay on the side of the state by the ocean. They drop their water on the west side of the mountains.

Find the Answers

1. A **peak** must be a

   a. state.

   b. wet side.

   c. rain cloud.

   d. mountaintop.

2. Most likely, much of the water in the clouds comes from the

   a. ocean.

   b. winds.

   c. dry side of the state.

   d. Cascade Mountains.

3. What side of Washington is by the ocean?

   a. east

   b. west

   c. north

   d. south

/3

Warm-Up 18

Name _____

The Biggest Country

There are a lot of countries in the world. There are almost two hundred. Some countries are big. Others are small. Russia is the biggest. No other country is bigger. Russia has the most land.

Russia is first. Canada is second when it comes to land. Still, Canada

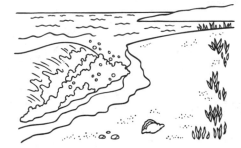 has something that is first. What is it? It is not land. It is a **coastline**. Canada has the longest in the world.

A coastline is land by the sea. It can be on an island. It can be on a mainland.

Find the Answers

1. Where would you find a **coastline**?

   a. at the store   c. in your house

   b. at the beach   d. in your school

2. From only the story, what can you tell about the coastline of the U.S.A.?

   a. It is as long as Russia's.   c. It is not as long as Russia's.

   b. It is as long as Canada's.   d. It is not as long as Canada's.

3. List these countries in order from big to small in land: Canada, Mexico, and Russia.

   a. Russia, Canada, Mexico   c. Mexico, Russia, Canada

   b. Mexico, Canada, Russia   d. Canada, Mexico, Russia

/3

Name _____

Warm-Up
19   **A State That Grows**

There are fifty states. One of the states is growing. It is getting bigger. What state is it? How can it grow?

It is Hawaii. Hawaii is made up of islands. It has more than one hundred islands. People live on some. They live on eight of the islands. The others are too small.

The biggest island is called Hawaii. It has a big volcano. The volcano is called Mauna Loa. Mauna Loa still erupts. Lava shoots out. The lava is hot. It flows down to the ocean. It hits the water. It is cooled by the water. It turns to rock. The island gets bigger!

Find the Answers

1. How many islands do people in Hawaii live on?

a. five   c. seven

b. six   d. eight

2. The biggest island

a. is no longer growing.   c. has the same name as the state.

b. is too small to live on.   d. has less than one hundred people living
                                    on it.

3. When a volcano shoots out lava, the volcano

a. cools.   c. gets bigger.

b. erupts.   d. turns to rock.

/3

Warm-Up 20

Name _____

A Strange Find

A scientist was in Montana. He was high up in the mountains. He was on a glacier. He saw something. It was very **strange**. It was ice that looked like elephant skin. What could it be?

The scientist dug into the ice. He did not find elephant skin. He found grasshoppers! Lots and lots of them! They had been trapped in the glacier for more than three hundred years!

How did this happen? Scientists think a sudden storm came up. It came up when the grasshoppers were flying in the area.

Find the Answers

1. Most likely, the scientist
   a. had seen elephant skin before.
   b. had never seen an elephant before.
   c. had been in the area three hundred years ago.
   d. had known what he would find in the ice.

2. Where was the glacier?
   a. Maine   c. Missouri
   b. Montana   d. Mississippi

3. What word means the same as **strange**?
   a. cold   c. sudden
   b. high   d. odd

/3

Name _____

Warm-Up 21

What They Race in Qatar

Qatar is a desert country. It is very hot. People like to race in Qatar. They do not race cars. They do not race horses. They do not race dogs. What do they race? They race a desert animal. They race camels!

Small children used to ride the camels. It was too dangerous. Who rides the camels now? Robots do! The robots are **remote-controlled**. They are controlled by someone watching the race.

The robots have on sunglasses. They wear hats. They smell of perfume. Why do they have on sunglasses? Why do they wear hats? Why do they smell of perfume? It makes the robots seem human. Then the camels are not afraid of the robots.

Find the Answers

1. Most likely, if there are more sandstorms than rainstorms,

  a. it rains a lot.

  b. it is not a desert.

  c. it is a desert.

  d. it is a land without animals.

2. Which of the following cannot be **remote-controlled**?

  a. a TV

  b. a toy racecar

  c. a CD player

  d. a baby

3. What is *not* true about the robots?

  a. They wear hats.

  b. They wear socks.

  c. They wear sunglasses.

  d. They smell of perfume.

/3

Name _____

Warm-Up 22

Airport Island

Japan needed to build a new airport. There was a problem. There was not enough space. The land was too crowded. People thought and thought. They came up with an answer.

The answer was to build an island. They would build an island in a bay. Building the island was a lot of work. It took a long time. Three mountains were **leveled**. The dirt from the mountains was used to make the island.

The new island was big enough for the airport. When it was done, a bridge was built. The bridge connected the new island to the old Japan.

Find the Answers

1. When something is **leveled,** it is

   a. crowded.

   b. connected.

   c. made flat.

   d. built in a bay.

2. Dirt from how many mountains was used to make the new island?

   a. three

   b. four

   c. five

   d. six

3. The bridge had to be built so

   a. there was more space.

   b. an answer could be found.

   c. people would be less crowded.

   d. people could easily get to the airport.

/3

Warm-Up 23

Name _____

Too Wet for a Race

A race is held once a year. It is a boat race. It is held on the Todd River. One year, the race was **canceled**. Why was the race canceled? There was water in the river!

The race is in Australia. It is in the outback. The outback is very dry. It is a desert. It rains very little. The Todd River is usually dry. Its riverbed is nothing but sand. People take boats. They cut out the bottoms and race with the boats. They do not paddle them. They carry them while running!

In 1993, it rained in the outback. Water flowed in the river. The race had to be canceled because it was too wet!

Find the Answers

1. If something is no longer done, it is

   a. canceled.   c. nothing but sand.

   b. usually dry.   d. held once a year.

2. What might be another title for the story?

   a. "Racing in the Rain"   c. "How Much It Rained in 1993"

   b. "Rivers in Australia"   d. "A Boat Race Without Paddling"

3. What is *not* true about the race?

   a. It takes place in Australia.   c. It takes place in the desert.

   b. It takes place in the water.   d. It takes place in the outback.

/3

Warm-Up
24

Name _____

A Name That Was a Trick

Greenland is an island. It is the largest island in the world. Greenland's name makes you think the island is green and **fertile**. It makes you think lots of things can grow on it.

Greenland is not green. It does not have fertile soil. Few plants can grow on it. In fact, most of Greenland is covered in ice.

The name was a trick. Eric the Red was a Viking. He sailed to the island in 983. He wanted people to come. He wanted people to settle. He knew more people would come if they thought the land was good for farming.

Find the Answers

1. When something is **fertile**, it is

a. not green.

b. covered in ice.

c. not good for farming.

d. good for growing things.

2. Who named the island?

a. Eric the Red

b. Eric the Blue

c. Eric the Green

d. Eric the Orange

3. A store is called "The Sweet Shop." Most likely, the name makes you think of

a. worms.

b. candy.

c. pepper.

d. bedbugs.

/3

Name _____

Warm-Up 25

A Bridge to Jump Off

The New River Gorge Bridge is in West Virginia. The bridge is very high. It crosses a deep gorge. One day a year, something is allowed. It is the only time it is allowed. What can people do on this one day?

People can jump off the bridge. They can use parachutes. They can use bungee cords. They can use ropes. Not anyone can jump. Only people who have jumped before can jump. They must have jumped at least fifty times. The jumps could be from planes or buildings.

People come to watch, too. They watch people parachute off the bridge. They look at people using bungee cords. They watch people slide down on ropes.

Find the Answers

1. Where is the bridge?

   a. New Mexico   c. West Virginia

   b. South Dakota   d. North Carolina

2. A narrow valley between steep cliffs is a

   a. rope.   c. parachute.

   b. gorge.   d. bungee cord.

3. What person could jump off the bridge?

   a. someone who has jumped one time before

   b. someone who has jumped eight times before

   c. someone who has jumped ten times before

   d. someone who has jumped eighty times before

/3

Name _____

Warm-Up
26   **Idaho Before the Moon**

Astronauts were going far away. They were going to the moon. Before they went to the moon, they did something. They went to a place. The place was close. It was not as far as the moon.

Where did they go? They went to Idaho.

A park is in Idaho. Its name is Craters of the Moon. Long ago, volcanoes erupted in the park. Lava flowed out. Today, the lava is like an ocean of hard rock. Craters dot the park. The astronauts went to the park to study its landscape. They went to get ready for the moon.

Find the Answers

1. Most likely, one thing the astronauts found on the moon was

  a. a park.

  b. a crater.

  c. an ocean.

  d. flowing lava.

2. *Close* is to *far* as

  a. *hard* is to *dot*.

  b. *hard* is to *long*.

  c. *hard* is to *flow*.

  d. *hard* is to *soft*.

3. Lava flows out when

  a. a volcano erupts.

  b. a place is close.

  c. astronauts go to Idaho.

  d. astronauts go to the moon.

/3

**Warm-Up
27**

Name _____

A Gray Suit

The Sydney Harbor Bridge is in Australia. It is big and tall. There is a special way to see the bridge. You can climb it! You step over girders. You duck under and squeeze through girders. You climb stairs. You go up high!

Before you climb, you have to put on a suit. The suit covers your clothes. The suit has two shades. It has two shades of gray. The gray suit matches the bridge. It makes you **blend in**.

Wearing the suit, you don't stand out. People can look at the bridge. People can drive on the bridge. They pay attention to the view and the road. They don't pay attention to you.

Find the Answers

1. The bridge must be what color?

a. tan

b. gold

c. blue

d. gray

2. When you **blend in**, you

a. climb stairs.

b. don't stand out.

c. step over girders.

d. pay attention to the road.

3. Most likely, drivers are safer if they

a. pay attention to the road.

b. pay attention to the view.

c. pay attention to the stairs.

d. pay attention to the girders.

/3

Name _____

Warm-Up
28   **A Famous Tower**

A famous tower is in France. It is in the city of Paris. It was built in 1889. It is made of iron. It is very high. It has lots of steps. It has more than 1,500 steps. It is called the Eiffel Tower.

People come to see the tower. They come from all over. They want to go up the tower. They want to go up high. They want to look out over the city.

People have two ways to go up. They can walk up the tower. They can take an elevator. It costs less to walk. It costs more to ride the elevator. How would you go up?

Find the Answers

1. Most likely, how many ways can you safely go down the tower?

    a. one   c. three

    b. two   d. four

2. What is the Eiffel Tower made of?

    a. wood   c. iron

    b. rock   d. steel

3. A person would pay less to go up the tower if he or she

    a. had come from France.   c. wanted to look out over the city.

    b. wanted to ride the elevator.   d. did not mind walking up lots of steps.

/3

Name _____

Warm-Up
29

A House on Stilts

You go to a small village. The village is in Vietnam. It is away from the big city. It is in the country. The house is made of wood. It is built on stilts. Why is the house up on stilts? Why is it high above the ground?

Vietnam has a rainy season. The waters rise. Land floods. The house on stilts is safe from the water. It stays dry inside.

Houses on stilts also keep out vermin. Vermin are small pests. Rats are a kind of vermin. Mice are a kind of vermin. It is easier to keep vermin out when a house is on stilts.

Find the Answers

1. What answer is *not* vermin?

   a. lice   c. goats

   b. flies   d. bedbugs

2. What is most likely true about Vietnam's rainy season?

   a. It rains a lot.   c. It rains after it snows.

   b. It rains only a little.   d. It does not happen very often.

3. At times, people could use the space under the house to

   a. work with vermin.   c. work out in the sun.

   b. work in the shade.   d. work above the ground.

/3

Warm-Up 30

Name _____

Day and Night Are the Same

There is a place where it is always the same temperature. It is the same in summer and fall. It is the same in winter and spring. It is the same in the day and night. It is the same all the time.

It is always dark. It is dark all the time. You cannot see your hand. Put your hand in front of your face. You still can't see it! Where could this place be?

It is Mammoth Cave. This cave is in Kentucky. The cave is big and deep. The sun's heat does not warm the inside air. It is always 54°F. The sun's light cannot enter the cave. It is always pitch-black.

Find the Answers

1. If someone saw his or her hand in Mammoth Cave, most likely,

a. the sun was shining.

b. it was a summer day.

c. he or she was holding a light.

d. the hand was close to his or her face.

2. Many animals that live in the cave are blind. Most likely, this is because

a. eyes are not useful.

b. legs are not useful.

c. arms are not useful.

d. noses are not useful.

3. What answer is true about the temperature in the cave?

a. It is warmer in summer than winter.

b. It is warmer in spring than fall.

c. It is cooler in spring than summer.

d. It is the same in winter and summer.

/3

Scientifically Speaking

Name _____

Warm-Up
1

The Most Bones

A baby has bones. An old person has bones. We all have bones. Bones hold us up. The biggest bone is in your leg. It is called the femur. The smallest bone is in your ear. It is called the stirrup.

Who has the most bones? Every old person has the same number of bones. How many bones do they have? They have 206 bones.

Babies have more bones than big people. They have about 300. As babies grow, some of their bones **fuse** together. Their 300 bones become 206 bones.

Find the Answers

1. What is the biggest bone called?

a. leg

c. femur

b. ear

d. stirrup

2. When something **fuses**, it

a. eats together.

c. plays together.

b. joins together.

d. reads together.

3. Why might a baby bend more easily than an old person?

a. It has fewer bones to hold it up.

c. It doesn't have any bones to hold it up.

b. All its bones are fused together.

d. All its bones aren't fused together yet.

/3

Warm-Up
2

Name _____

The Turtle's Tears

A sea turtle **sheds** tears. The tears are big and salty. Why does the sea turtle shed tears? Is the sea turtle sad?

The sea turtle is not sad. The sea turtle's tears are good. A sea turtle lives in the ocean. It drinks ocean water. The water is salty. Too much salt is not good for a turtle. Too much salt can make it die.

The sea turtle has a way to get rid of salt. What does the sea turtle do? It sheds tears! It sheds big, salty tears to get rid of extra salt.

Find the Answers

1. Where does a sea turtle get its water?

    a. from the sink
            c. from the ocean

    b. from the hose
           d. from the river

2. If a sea turtle drinks a lot of water, it will

    a. feel sad.
            c. not shed any tears.

    b. need more salt.
          d. shed a lot of tears.

3. When you **shed** something, you

    a. run or take it.
           c. eat or drink it.

    b. lose or drop it.
          d. cry or feel sad.

/3

Warm-Up 3

Name _____

Clam Drop

A gull is hungry. It wants to eat. The gull **scoops** up a clam. It wants to eat it. How can the gull eat the clam? The clam has a hard shell. The gull cannot break it open with its beak. The shell is tightly closed. The gull cannot open it.

The gull flies up with the clam. The gull flies high above a rock. Then the gull lets it go! The clam drops. It falls down, down, down to the rock below. It smashes on the rock, and the shell breaks apart.

The gull flies down fast! It scoops up the clam meat. It eats the clam it could not open.

Find the Answers

1. When you **scoop** something, you
   - a. break it.
   - b. fly fast.
   - c. fall down.
   - d. pick it up.

2. The gull could not break the clam with its beak because
   - a. the gull was too hungry.
   - b. the clam's shell was too hard.
   - c. the rocks were too far below.
   - d. the meat was smashed on the rock.

3. Most likely, if a gull eats clam meat,
   - a. rocks are close by.
   - b. the clam is hungry.
   - c. there are no rocks.
   - d. the gull falls down.

/3

Warm-Up 4

The Longest and the Shortest Days

Name _____

You live on Earth. Earth is a planet. It **rotates**. It turns and spins. What is a day? A day is the time it takes a planet to spin around. On Earth, a day is 24 hours.

Venus is a planet. It rotates. It turns slowly. How long does it take to spin around? It takes 243 Earth days! One day on Venus is 243 days on Earth. Venus is the planet with the longest day.

Venus

Jupiter is a planet. It rotates. It turns fast. Jupiter spins around in less than ten Earth hours. Jupiter has two days for every one day on Earth! Jupiter is the planet with the shortest day.

Jupiter

Find the Answers

1. One day on Venus is how many Earth days?

a. 240 days   c. 242 days

b. 241 days   d. 243 days

2. From the story, you can tell that

a. Venus turns faster than Earth.

b. Venus turns faster than Jupiter.

c. Jupiter turns faster than Venus.

d. Jupiter turns slower than Earth.

3. If something **rotates**, it

a. spins around.   c. is less than a day.

b. takes 24 hours.   d. has the longest day.

/3

Name _____

Warm-Up
5

The Hungry Shark

A shark is hungry. The hungry shark sees a big fish. The shark is fast. The shark grabs the big fish and eats it. The hungry shark sees a bigger fish. The shark is fast. It eats the bigger fish. The hungry shark sees an even bigger fish. The shark is fast. It eats the even bigger fish. The shark eats every fish that it sees. Not one fish can get away.

Then the shark sees a little fish. The little fish is called a Moses sole. The shark bites down. What happens? The little fish lets out a milky poison. The milky poison hurts the shark. The shark opens its mouth. It lets the little fish go!

Find the Answers

1. Why doesn't the shark eat the little fish?

   a. The little fish is fast.   c. The shark sees a bigger fish.

   b. The shark is not hungry.   d. The little fish lets out a poison.

2. What is the name of the little fish?

   a. Moses seed   c. Roses seed

   b. Moses sole   d. Roses sole

3. Most likely, the poison is what color?

   a. blue   c. white

   b. green   d. yellow

/3

Warm-Up 6

Name _____

The First Refrigerator

Long ago, people had to dry their food. They had to smoke their food. They had to pickle their food. They had to salt their food. If they didn't, the food would **rot**. It would spoil.

Later, people began to use ice. They had large boxes. They would put in a block of ice. An iceman would bring the ice. The ice would keep the food cold. It would keep the food from spoiling.

The first electric refrigerator was invented in 1913. It did not need ice to keep the food cool. Over time, inventors changed the design. They made it better. Today, refrigerators do not need ice. They can make ice!

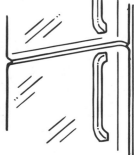

Find the Answers

1. Long ago, to keep food from spoiling, people did all but what to it?

a. dry it   c. smoke it

b. salt it   d. design it

2. What year was the electric refrigerator invented?

a. 1319   c. 1913

b. 1519   d. 1915

3. What word means nearly the same as **rot**?

a. cool   c. change

b. spoil   d. invent

/3

Name _____

Warm-Up 7

A True Super Suit

You are wearing a true super suit. This suit protects you. It guards your body from the outside world. It keeps germs out. It is waterproof. It can mend itself.

This suit fits you perfectly. It will always fit you perfectly. It will never be too small. It will never be too big. It can stretch and grow. What is this super suit? It is your skin!

Where does a lot of dust in your house come from? Believe it or not, it comes from your skin! Skin cells **flake off** all the time. They flake off by the thousands. New skin cells keep growing back.

Find the Answers

1. What is *not* a reason your skin is a super suit?

    a. It is waterproof.   c. It turns into dust.

    b. It can mend itself.   d. It will never be too big.

2. The title that sums up the story best is

    a. "All About Skin."   c. "All About Cells."

    b. "All About Dust."   d. "All About Germs."

3. When something **flakes off**, it comes off in

    a. fat, heavy pieces.   c. wide, thick pieces.

    b. big, chunky pieces.   d. small, thin pieces.

/3

Warm-Up

8   **A Snake That Can Catch a Bat**

Name _____

Bats fly. Snakes crawl. How can a snake catch a bat? The boa constrictor is a snake. It lives where it is warm. It lives in **tropical** areas. The boa slithers up a tree. It hangs from a limb. It can catch a bat as it flies by!

Boas eat things besides bats. They eat rats, lizards, and monkeys. How do boas kill their prey? They constrict them! They wrap themselves around animals. They squeeze. They squeeze tighter and tighter.

Find the Answers

1. From the story, you can tell that a **tropical** area is

   a. warm.   c. a zoo.

   b. cold.   d. a lake.

2. If you put on a shirt that is too small, it might make you feel as if you were

   a. flying.   c. slithering.

   b. crawling.   d. constricted.

3. You might *not* know what the story's main idea was if

   a. you only read the title.   c. you only read the first paragraph.

   b. you only read the first sentence.   d. you only read the second paragraph.

/3

Name _____

Warm-Up 9

What the Owl Throws Up

Once or twice a day, an owl gets rid of something. It comes out of the owl's mouth. The owl throws it up. The owl regurgitates it. Why does the owl do this? What does it regurgitate?

An owl can't chew its food. It doesn't have the right teeth. An owl tears its food apart. It swallows big pieces. The pieces have bones and hair. They have fur.

The owl can't digest bones or hair. It can't digest fur. These have to come out. The bones, hair, and fur get packed into a pellet. The owl throws up the pellet. It regurgitates it.

Find the Answers

1. Why can't an owl chew its food?

   a. It can swallow bones.   c. It only has teeth for tearing.

   b. It can digest fur and hair.   d. It doesn't have hands to hold it.

2. From the story, you can tell that an owl eats

   a. grass.   c. plants.

   b. animals.   d. flowers.

3. When an animal coughs something up, it

   a. chews it.   c. swallows it.

   b. digests it.   d. regurgitates it.

/3

Name _____

Warm-Up 10

Why Astronauts Sneeze

Astronauts in space can sneeze a lot. They can sneeze more than one hundred times a day! Why do they sneeze a lot? What makes them sneeze so many times?

Dust does not settle in space. It floats in the air. It gets into the astronauts' noses. It makes the astronauts sneeze and sneeze.

Dust settles on Earth. Why doesn't it settle in space? Why does it float in the air? Astronauts in space are far away. They do not feel Earth's gravity. There is not enough gravity to pull the dust down. Earth's gravity is a force. It draws us toward Earth's center.

Find the Answers

1. The story says that astronauts in space can sneeze

   a. less than ten times a day.

   b. more than one hundred times a day.

   c. less than one hundred times a day.

   d. more than one thousand times a day.

2. What can you tell about astronauts in space from the story?

   a. They float in space.   c. They do not sneeze a lot.

   b. They are close to Earth.   d. They are pulled down by Earth's gravity.

3. When an astronaut is on Earth, he or she most likely

   a. never sneezes.   c. sneezes less than you do.

   b. sneezes more than you do.   d. sneezes about the same as you do.

/3

Warm-Up

11

Name _____

Popcorn

How does popcorn pop? What makes the kernels open up? The answer is water!

A corn kernel has a hard outer shell. It has a starchy inside. Starch is a plant's stored food. All green plants make starch. What's inside the kernel's starchy center? A small dab of water is inside.

Something happens to the water when the kernel is heated. The water turns into steam. The steam expands. It pushes out. It is like a balloon. The shell can't take it! Pop! The shell bursts! The kernel turns inside out! The starchy inside is now on the outside. It is the white part of the popcorn.

Find the Answers

1. A corn kernel will only turn into popcorn if there is
a. heat.   c. a shell.
b. food.   d. a balloon.

2. What is a kernel made of, from the outside to the inside?
a. a dab of water, a hard shell, starch
b. starch, a dab of water, a hard shell
c. a hard shell, a dab of water, starch
d. a hard shell, starch, a dab of water

3. What does every green plant make?
a. water   c. starch
b. steam   d. kernels

/3

Warm-Up

12

Name _____

Why Spiders Don't Get Stuck

Spiders spin silk. They can spin different kinds. Some silk is sticky. Other silk is not sticky. A spider's web looks like it has spokes. The spokes are not sticky. The spider makes this part first. Next, the spider adds sticky **strands.**

Insects get trapped in the web's sticky strands. The spider quickly swings across the web. It goes to the insect. Why doesn't the spider get stuck?

The spider has special claws. It uses its claws to hook to the web and swing to the non-sticky strands.

What if the spider slips? What if it gets stuck on a sticky strand? The spider has a special oil. The oil helps to keep it from getting stuck.

Find the Answers

1. A **strand** is like a

  a. thread.   c. window.

  b. pillow.   d. fire truck.

2. The spokes of a spider's webs are

  a. not made first.   c. made with a special oil.

  b. made with sticky silk.   d. made with non-sticky silk.

3. What does a spider use to hook itself to its web?

  a. oil   c. claws

  b. tape   d. ropes

/3

Warm-Up
13

Name _____

The Most Kinds

You are a mammal. A dog and a cat are mammals. A snake is a reptile. A turtle and a lizard are reptiles. A robin is a bird. An emu and a hawk are birds. A trout is a fish. A cod and a salmon are fish. A fly is an insect. A beetle and a cricket are insects.

What kind of living thing is there the most of? Are there more mammals? Are there more reptiles? Are there more birds? Are there more fish? Are there more insects?

There are more kinds of insects in the world than anything else. One time, a person counted beetles. The person counted 1,200 kinds of beetles in just nineteen trees!

Find the Answers

1. What is *not* a reptile?

    a. a snake   c. a lizard

    b. a turtle   d. a cricket

2. How many trees did the person count beetles in?

    a. nine   c. ninety-one

    b. nineteen   d. twenty-nine

3. What answer do you know is true?

    a. There are more birds than insects.

    b. There are more reptiles than fish.

    c. There are more insects than mammals.

    d. There are more mammals than reptiles.

/3

Name _____

Warm-Up
14   **The Quiet Flyer**

An owl is a bird. An owl can fly very quietly. It can swoop down on its prey. Its prey doesn't hear the owl coming. How can an owl fly so quietly?

The feathers on the edges of an owl's wing are very soft. The soft edges muffle the sound of the owl's wings moving. Not all birds have wings with such soft edges. Their sounds are not muffled.

You can see for yourself how soft edges muffle sound. Take a soft tissue. Take a piece of paper. Wave the tissue in the air. Then wave the piece of paper. Listen carefully. The soft tissue makes less noise.

Find the Answers

1. When something is made *less* loud or clear,

a. it is waved.   c. it is muffled.

b. it is moved.   d. it swoops down.

2. Most likely, what would make the *least* noise if you waved it in the air?

a. a book   c. a wooden board

b. a kite   d. a piece of ribbon

3. What part of an owl's wing feathers are soft?

a. the back   c. the front

b. the edges   d. the middle

/3

Name _____

Warm-Up 15

Different Seasons

Julie said, "It is July 15th. It is hot. It is summer. I will wear shorts. I will wear a sun hat and sandals."

Jay said, "It is July 15th. It is cold. It is winter. I will wear a coat. I will wear a warm hat and boots."

Julie and Jay were both right. How could this be? Julie lived in the north. Jay lived in the south. Seasons are different at the ends of Earth. When it is summer in one place, it is winter in the other. This is because of the way Earth tilts as it goes around the sun.

Find the Answers

1. What season was Julie in?

   a. fall

   b. spring

   c. summer

   d. winter

2. If it is summer in South America, it is most likely

   a. fall in North America.

   b. winter in North America.

   c. spring in North America.

   d. summer in North America.

3. Most likely, Jay and Julie were

   a. living in the same city.

   b. going to the same school.

   c. sitting next to each other.

   d. very far away from each other.

/3

Warm-Up
16

Name _____

The Place to Throw Far

You are in the Rocky Mountains. You are up high. You are on top of a mountain. You throw a ball.

You are in Death Valley. You are down low. You are below sea level. You throw a ball.

Where does the ball go farther? Is it easier to throw far up high or down low? The ball will go farther in the mountains. The higher you are above sea level, the thinner the air gets. Up high, there is less air to hold the ball back.

Find the Answers

1. Why might you have trouble breathing in the Rocky Mountains?

   a. The valley is high.   c. It is below sea level.

   b. The air is thinner.   d. It is hard to throw a ball.

2. *Far* is to *near* as

   a. *jump* is to *hop*.   c. *hot* is to *cold*.

   b. *cry* is to *weep*.   d. *sleep* is to *nap*.

3. Where is it below sea level?

   a. Death Valley   c. Rocky Mountains

   b. Canary Island   d. White Mountains

/3

Warm-Up
17

Name _____

Plant Trap

A pitcher plant eats insects. How does the pitcher plant get its food? It drowns it!

Pitcher plants are traps. The plants are shaped like a pitcher or jug. There is liquid at the bottom of the **jug**. The plant makes nectar. The nectar is sweet. The nectar is around the rim of the jug. The rim is slippery.

Insects want the nectar. When they land on the slippery rim, they slip in. They fall to the bottom. They land in the liquid. They drown. The insect becomes a meal for the plant.

Find the Answers

1. A **jug** is a kind of

   a. plant.   c. nectar.

   b. liquid.   d. pitcher.

2. How does the pitcher plant get insects to come to it?

   a. It makes nectar.   c. It makes a meal.

   b. It makes a trap.   d. It makes a liquid.

3. Where is the rim?

   a. in the pitcher's middle   c. around the plant's bottom

   b. around the pitcher's top   d. in the liquid at the bottom

/3

Name _____

What the Rings Tell

How do you know how old a tree is? You can count its rings. There is one ring for each year.

You can tell more than a tree's age from its rings. What can you tell? You can see how much a tree has grown. Look at the size of each ring. Some rings are very close to each other. Other rings are farther apart.

A tree may grow only a little if there is not enough water. It may grow only a little if it is too cold or hot. It will have small rings. If the weather is nice, the tree may grow more. Its rings on good years will be bigger.

Find the Answers

1. If a tree has ten rings, you know for sure that the tree

    a. is ten years old.   c. grew in nice weather.

    b. is one hundred years old.   d. grew when it was hot.

2. A tree that is the same age as you will

    a. be bigger than you.

    b. be smaller than you.

    c. have the same number rings as your age.

    d. have two times more rings than your age.

3. Most likely, if there is little water for many years, the tree will have

    a. fewer rings than if it was wet.   c. some rings that are far apart.

    b. more rings than if it was wet.   d. some rings that are close together.

/3

Warm-Up

19

Name _____

Impossible to Sink

The Great Salt Lake is in Utah. You can swim in the lake. You can float in it. It is almost impossible to sink in it. Try to sink and you just bob up and down. Why can't you sink?

The Great Salt Lake is very salty. It is four times as salty as the ocean. Salt water is denser than fresh water. When something is dense, its parts are very close together. The "thicker" salt water holds you up. The salt water's density makes it almost impossible to sink.

See for yourself. Fill a glass with water. Put in an egg. The egg will sink. Add in lots of salt. The egg will float!

Find the Answers

1. Air is less dense than water. This makes

    a. running on land and water the same.

    b. running easier in water than on land.

    c. it easier to walk through air than water.

    d. it harder to walk through air than water.

2. Which of the following statements is true?

    a. The ocean is saltier than the Great Salt Lake.

    b. The Great Salt Lake is two times as salty as the ocean.

    c. The Great Salt Lake is three times as salty as the ocean.

    d. The Great Salt Lake is four times as salty as the ocean.

3. When something is very hard to do, it may seem as if it is

    a. very salty.   c. very dense.

    b. impossible.   d. bobbing up and down.

/3

Warm-Up 20

How to Tell the Oldest Mountains

Name _____

You see two mountain ranges. One range is filled with peaks. The peaks are high. They are rugged. They have steep sides. The mountains in the other range are smoother. They are not as high. They are not as rugged. Which mountains are older? Which ones are younger? How can you tell?

The smoother mountains are older. The range with the higher, more rugged peaks is younger. This is because mountains get worn away. Over time, they are **eroded**. They are eroded by water and rain. They are eroded by ice and wind. The water, rain, ice, and wind smoothes the mountains. It wears them down.

Find the Answers

1. When something is **eroded**, it is

   a. higher.   c. younger.

   b. steeper.   d. worn away.

2. A group of mountains makes up a

   a. town.   c. range.

   b. peak.   d. steep side.

3. The Rocky Mountains have high, rugged peaks. The Appalachian Mountains are smoother and more rounded. What answer is true?

   a. The Appalachian Mountains are older than the Rocky Mountains.

   b. The Rocky Mountains are older than the Appalachian Mountains.

   c. The Appalachian Mountains are younger than the Rocky Mountains.

   d. The Rocky Mountains and the Appalachian Mountains are the same age.

/3

Warm-Up 21

Name _____

Twinkling Stars

Look up at night. You will see stars. The stars twinkle. They seem to change brightness all the time. The truth is that stars do not twinkle. They only look as if they are twinkling.

Stars give off a **steady** light. They shine steadily. Their light hits Earth's atmosphere. Then something happens. Air currents do something to the light. They make it bend. Some light gets into our eyes. Some light is bent away. It looks to us as if the stars are twinkling.

Find the Answers

1. From the story, you can tell that
   a. light can be bent.
   b. light cannot be bent.
   c. light cannot come from far away.
   d. light cannot go through Earth's atmosphere.

2. If something is **steady**, it
   a. is very hot.
   b. stops and goes.
   c. is not very hot.
   d. does not stop and go.

3. Most likely, if you were above Earth's atmosphere, a star's light would
   a. seem to be dark.
   b. seem to twinkle more.
   c. seem to shine steadily.
   d. seem to change brightness all the time.

/3

Warm-Up

22

Name _____

Dinosaur Fossils

Dinosaurs lived long ago. How do we know about them?
We look for fossils. A **fossil** is the remains of a plant
or animal.

How were dinosaurs born? We did not know. Then in
1923, we knew. A fossil was found. It was a dinosaur egg!
Many more eggs have been found since then. Some were found in nests.

Did some dinosaurs sit on their eggs? We did not know. Then in 1993,
we knew. A fossil was found. It was a dinosaur fossil. It was sitting on a
nest. The nest was filled with eggs! The dinosaur was sitting on the eggs to
hatch them.

Find the Answers

1. What animal today can hatch their babies like some dinosaurs?

a. a cat   c. a bird

b. a dog   d. a hamster

2. What year was the *first* dinosaur egg found?

a. 1823   c. 1893

b. 1923   d. 1993

3. What might be a **fossil**?

a. a book that is ripped

b. a bike you are too big for now

c. a bird that is flying in the sky

d. a bone of a cat that lived long ago

/3

Name _____

Warm-Up 23

Claws of the Fastest

Cats have claws. The claws go in and out. Only one cat has claws that do not go in and out. The claws stay out. What cat has claws that stay out? It is a big cat. The big cat has spots. It is the fastest cat. It is the cheetah.

The cheetah's claws help it go fast. The claws are like cleats on shoes. Shoe cleats dig into the ground. They keep a runner from slipping. A cheetah springs into a fast run. It does not slip. Its sharp claws keep it from slipping.

Find the Answers

1. What answer is *false?*

   a. A cheetah has no spots.   c. A cheetah can spring fast.

   b. A cheetah has sharp claws.   d. A cheetah is the fastest cat.

2. A tiger is a cat. A tiger's claws

   a. stay in.   c. are not sharp.

   b. stay out.   d. go in and out.

3. Most likely, cleats are *not* on school shoes because they would

   a. make you run too fast.   c. keep you from slipping.

   b. dig into the floor.   d. make you spring into a run.

/3

Name _____

Warm-Up

24 | **The Darker Hand**

Try something. Stand up. Put one arm straight down. Raise the other arm up, straight up. Hold it high in the air. Keep your arms straight up and down. Don't move them. Hold them for one whole minute.

Then put your hands in front of you. Look at them. One of them will be darker than the other!

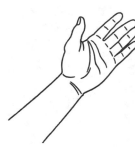 Your blood is dark. It is red. It **flows** through your body. It is pumped by your heart. When your hand is held high, blood drains easily to the heart. When your hand is held low, it is harder for the blood to flow back to the heart. The blood collects in the hand. It makes the hand darker.

Find the Answers

1. This story is mainly about

    a. standing up.   c. your heart pumping.

    b. the flow of blood.   d. what your hands are for.

2. When something **flows** out, it

    a. fills out.   c. drains out.

    b. pumps out.   d. collects out.

3. It is harder for the blood to flow back to the heart in the hand that is held down because

    a. the heart is above the hand.   c. the heart is in back of the hand.

    b. the heart is below the hand.   d. the heart is in front of the hand.

/3

Warm-Up 25

Name _____

Blue Blood

A dog has red blood. A cat has red blood. You have red blood. A lobster does not have red blood. It has blue blood! Why does a lobster have blue blood instead of red blood?

Our blood is made of more than one thing. It has plasma. Plasma is light yellow. It has white blood cells. It has red blood cells. We have lots and lots of red blood cells. All the red blood cells make our blood look red.

Our red blood cells have hemoglobin. Hemoglobin makes the blood cells red. Lobster blood cells do not have hemoglobin.

Find the Answers

1. What can you tell about a dog's blood from this story?

   a. It has hemoglobin.

   b. It is the same as a lobster's.

   c. It has more plasma than our blood.

   d. It has fewer white blood cells than a cat.

2. Our blood looks red because it has

   a. cells.

   b. plasma.

   c. a lobster.

   d. hemoglobin.

3. Without red blood cells, human blood most likely looks

   a. blue.

   b. brown.

   c. yellow.

   d. orange.

/3

Warm-Up 26

Name _____

Wolf Den

A mother wolf has her pups in a den. The den is under the ground. It is often dug into the side of a hill. The den has a tunnel. The tunnel always slopes up. The tunnel goes to a chamber, or room. The chamber is where the pups are born.

Why does the tunnel to the chamber slope up? This is to keep the pups dry. Water does not run uphill. If it rains, the water goes down the side of the hill. It does not go into the chamber where the pups are nesting.

Find the Answers

1. *Wolf* is to *pup* as

   a. *dog* is to *bark.*

   b. *fox* is to *tail.*

   c. *bird* is to *fly.*

   d. *cat* is to *kitten.*

2. A flat road

   a. would slope up.

   b. would slope down.

   c. would have no slope.

   d. would have a slope in the middle.

3. A judge's chambers would be

   a. rooms where the judge works.

   b. the clothes the judge wears.

   c. a tunnel to the judge's desk.

   d. the people who come to see the judge.

/3

Name _____

Doctors Who Spread Germs

Long ago, doctors would treat sick people. They would go from one sick person to the next. The doctors would not wash their hands. They did not change their clothes. They did not clean their tools. They did not wash up!

The doctors spread germs! Sometimes, they would make people sicker! At that time, people did not know about germs. They did not know how sickness was spread.

A doctor named Lister read a new study. It was about germs. Lister began to wash his hands. He began to clean his tools. His patients did not get sicker. They got better. Now all doctors do what Lister did.

Find the Answers

1. From the story, you can tell that

   a. germs are not easily spread.   c. washing up helps to spread germs.

   b. germs do not make people sick.   d. washing up can stop the spread
                                               of germs.

2. Someone who goes to see a doctor is the doctor's

   a. plate.   c. patient.

   b. paper.   d. passenger.

3. Most likely, doctors did not know about germs long ago because they did *not*

   a. know how to read.   c. care about sick people.

   b. have a way to see them.   d. have a lot of tools to wash.

/3

Name _____

Warm-Up
28   **Why We Burp**

We know what to say after burping. We say, "Excuse me." But do we know what a burp is? Do we know why we burp?

A burp is nothing but gas. We eat and we drink. We can't help but swallow air as we do this. Air is filled with gases. At times, our bodies need to get rid of some gas. Extra gas is forced out of the stomach. It goes up a tube. It goes up the same tube our food went down. It comes out of the mouth as a burp.

Find the Answers

1. Why might drinking fizzy soft drinks make you burp more?
   a. Soft drinks do not have any gas in them.
   b. Soft drinks have extra gas in them to make them fizzy.
   c. Soft drinks cannot be forced out of the stomach.
   d. Soft drinks do not go down the tube that our food goes down.

2. What should you say after burping?
   a. "Please leave."   c. "After you."
   b. "Thank you."   d. "Excuse me."

3. What is the correct order for what we do to our food?
   a. down the tube, swallow, in the stomach
   b. in the stomach, down the tube, swallow
   c. swallow, down the tube, in the stomach
   d. swallow, in the stomach, down the tube

/3

Name _____

Warm-Up 29

Make It Go One Hundred Miles an Hour!

Take a very small thing. It is so small you can't see it. You can make it go one hundred miles an hour! You do this all the time. How do you do it? You sneeze!

Something gets in your nose. It may be dust. It may be pollen. It **bothers** you. Your nose sends a message to your brain. Your brain tells your body what to do. It makes your muscles work together. It makes your muscles act in the right order. Your brain makes what is bothering you come flying out. What is bothering you comes out fast! It comes out when you sneeze.

Find the Answers

1. If something **bothers** you, it _____ you.

   a. upsets   c. surprises

   b. excites   d. quiets

2. Where does your nose send the message?

   a. to your body   c. to your brain

   b. to your face   d. to your muscles

3. Another title for this story might be

   a. "All About Muscles."   c. "How Your Brain Works."

   b. "All About Sneezing."   d. "Small Things That Go Slow."

/3

Name _____

**Warm-Up
30**

A Horse That Bolted

Isaac Newton had a great mind. He thought up new ideas. He wrote about gravity. He wrote about math and light. Newton was born in 1642. He died in 1727. One man who was alive at the same time wrote about Newton.

The man wrote that Newton was walking. He was going up a hill. He was leading his horse. He was reading. Newton held the horse's reins in his right hand. He held his book in his left hand.

Newton got to the top of the hill. He got a surprise. There was no horse! It had **bolted**! The reins were empty. Newton had been too busy reading to see!

Find the Answers

1. Newton did *not* write about

  a. math.   c. horses.

  b. light.   d. gravity.

2. When something **bolts**, it suddenly

  a. runs away.   c. rides a horse.

  b. reads a book.   d. writes a story.

3. Most likely, Newton would say that the book he was reading was

  a. very bad.   c. very dull.

  b. very good.   d. very silly.

/3

From the Past

Warm-Up 1

An Old Hairstyle

How do you wear your hair? Is it long? Is it short? Do you tie it back? Do you braid it? Do you put it in pigtails? Most likely, you do not have the same hairstyle as some boys and girls of long ago.

Long ago in Egypt, boys and girls had the same hairstyle. All the boys and girls had shaved heads. Only one lock of hair was left. It was behind an ear. It was braided. When did the boys and girls stop shaving their heads? When did they start having different hairstyles? Boys and girls stopped shaving their heads when they were about twelve years old.

Find the Answers

1. A child's braid in long-ago Egypt would be
a. behind an ear.
b. on top of a head.
c. in back of a head.
d. in front of an ear.

2. A boy and a girl in long-ago Egypt had different hairstyles. How old could they both be?
a. two years old
b. five years old
c. eight years old
d. fifteen years old

3. What is true about hairstyles?
a. They are always the same as long ago.
b. They are not always the same as long ago.
c. Boys and girls always have the same style.
d. Boys and girls always have different styles.

/3

Warm-Up 2

Name _____

Cleaning Without Soap

Greece is a country. People in Greece cared about sports. They started the Olympic Games. Greek athletes would run fast. They would work hard. They would try to win.

After working hard, the athletes would wash. They would get clean. The athletes did not use water. They did not use soap. How did the athletes get clean?

Oil

Before working hard, the athletes used **oil**. They put the oil all over their bodies. After working hard, they would use a scraper. They would scrape off the oil. They would scrape off the dirt that stuck to the oil.

Find the Answers

1. What did the Greek athletes do *first*?

   a. used soap

   b. put oil on

   c. scraped oil off

   d. washed with water

2. What type of games started in Greece?

   a. the Scraper Games

   b. the Country Games

   c. the Olympic Games

   d. the Athletic Games

3. From the story, you can tell that **oil** is

   a. hot.

   b. sweet.

   c. green.

   d. sticky.

/3

Warm-Up 3

Name _____

A Game with a Snake

Long ago, Iroquois children played a game. The game was played in the winter. It was played on snow. First, a track was made in the snow. Often, the track was made by dragging a log. Then the track was sprinkled with water. This made the track hard and icy.

Next, the children took a "snake." The snake was a polished stick. It was very long. Children would take turns throwing the "snake" down the track. They would see who could throw it the farthest. You had to have good aim. If you threw it crookedly, the "snake" would go off the track.

Find the Answers

1. You can tell that Iroquois children

   a. lived where it snowed.

   b. only played in the winter.

   c. did not have time to play games.

   d. liked summer games more than winter games.

2. This game might have helped hunters

   a. track deer.

   b. catch snakes.

   c. have good aim.

   d. throw crookedly.

3. Most likely, the "snake" was polished because

   a. an ugly stick slides more easily.

   b. a rough stick slides more easily.

   c. a smooth stick slides more easily.

   d. a pretty stick slides more easily.

/3

Warm-Up

4

Name _____

Birthday Count

You are born. A year goes by. You turn one.
Another year goes by. You turn two. Every year on
your birthday, you add a year.

What if you were born long ago in China? The day you were born you
were one! When did you turn two? You turned two on the first day of the
Chinese New Year. Every New Year, you added a year.

You could be two years old in two days! How could this be? You are born
on the last day of the year. You are one. The next day is the first day of
the New Year. You turn two! This New Year birthday count started long
ago, but many people still use it today.

Find the Answers

1. A baby was how old on the day it was born in long-ago China?

    a. zero years old   c. two years old

    b. one year old   d. three years old

2. Every baby in long-ago China added a year to its age on

    a. the day after they were born.

    b. the year after they were born.

    c. the first day of the Chinese New Year.

    d. the very last day of the Chinese New Year.

3. From the story, you can tell that

    a. people counted birthdays long ago.

    b. age is always counted the same way.

    c. a day and a year are the same thing.

    d. more people were born in China long ago.

/3

Warm-Up 5

Name _____

May You Sit?

Long ago, France was ruled by kings. One king was Louis XIV. King Louis XIV lived in a big palace. People had to follow rules in the palace. Some of the rules were about sitting.

Who could sit? Who had to stand? In the king's court, only the king or queen could sit on an armchair. The king's children and the king's brother could sit in a chair. Their chair could have a back, but it could not have arms. A duchess could sit on a padded stool.

What about everyone else? What about you? You could not sit. You had to stand!

Find the Answers

1. What country did King Louis XIV rule?

a. France

b. Mexico

c. England

d. Germany

2. In King Louis' court, if your chair had a back but no arms, you might be

a. a queen.

b. a duchess.

c. the king's cook.

d. the king's child.

3. Most likely, King Louis' throne

a. only had a back.

b. was a padded stool.

c. had a back and arms.

d. was too small to sit in.

/3

Warm-Up
6

Name _____

The Moat

There is a castle. A wall goes around the castle. A ditch is dug outside the wall. The ditch is deep. It goes all around the wall. The ditch is filled with water. What is the water-filled ditch called? It is a moat.

Why were the ditches dug? Why were they filled with water? The moats were for defense. The water helped stop people who were **attacking** the castle.

How did people who lived in the castle get across the moat? A drawbridge would be let down. People could come and go. What if the castle was attacked? The drawbridge would be pulled up.

Find the Answers

1. Where was the moat dug?

   a. inside the wall   c. inside the castle

   b. outside the wall   d. next to the castle

2. What word means the opposite of **attack**?

   a. ditch   c. defend

   b. castle   d. drawbridge

3. From the story, you can tell that a drawbridge

   a. can move.   c. was filled with water.

   b. goes around a castle.   d. was only used for defense.

/3

Name _____

The Hammock

Long ago, sailors did not have beds. They slept on the hard deck. Then sailors from Europe went to the Americas. They saw something new. They had never seen it before. It was a hammock.

The sailors liked the hammocks. They were light. They were soft. They did not take a lot of space. They could be taken down during the day. The sailors took hammocks back to Europe. They used them as beds. Soon, people all over the world began to use hammocks.

Find the Answers

1. Hammocks were first made in

   a. Asia.   c. Australia.

   b. Europe.   d. the Americas.

2. Sailors long ago might *not* have used beds because

   a. they had never seen them before.

   b. their ships didn't have enough space.

   c. they liked to sleep on the hard deck.

   d. they didn't want to take hammocks back to Europe.

3. This story is mainly about

   a. the hammock.   c. what sailors had.

   b. the Americas.   d. people all over the world.

/3

Warm-Up

8

Left Foot, Right Foot

 You have a left foot. You have a right foot. You have shoes for each foot. Your left foot has a left shoe. Your right foot has a right shoe.

Long ago, many shoes were not fitted. Soldiers and other people had **straight** shoes. They did not curve to the left. They did not curve to the right. They could be worn on either foot.

Straight shoes were easier and cheaper to make. You could replace them one at a time. If one began to wear on one side, you could switch feet. This would make the shoe last longer.

Find the Answers

1. A soldier long ago could make his shoes last longer by

    a. switching to fitted shoes.

    b. switching what foot he put them on.

    c. wearing them only on the left foot.

    d. wearing them only on the right foot.

2. If something is **straight**, it is *not*

    a. curved.   c. easier.

    b. longer.   d. cheaper.

3. What might make fitted shoes better than straight shoes?

    a. They are cheaper.   c. They are easier to make.

    b. They last longer.   d. They do not hurt your feet.

/3

Name _____

Warm-Up 9

How Many Knots?

A ship sails. It moves in the water. How fast does the ship go? We say it goes so many knots per hour. Why do we say knots? Why don't we use miles or meters?

Long ago, sailors would throw a small wood panel into the ocean. One end of a rope was on the panel. The other end of the rope was around a reel. The rope had knots on it. Each knot was the same distance apart.

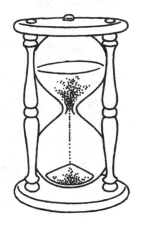

As the ship moved, the rope would unwind. A sailor would use a timer. He would count the knots. He would see how many knots the rope unwound in a set time.

Find the Answers

1. What was the rope wound on?

  a. a reel   c. a timer

  b. a knot   d. a panel

2. When we say how fast a ship goes, we say it goes

  a. feet per hour.   c. knots per hour.

  b. miles per hour.   d. meters per hour.

3. The fastest ships would go

  a. fewer knots per hour than slower ships.

  b. more knots per hour than slower ships.

  c. fewer knots per meter than slower ships.

  d. the same knots per hour as slower ships.

/3

Warm-Up

10

Name _____

Rescue Dogs

There was a high **pass**. It was called the Saint Bernard Pass. It was in the Swiss Alps. In the winter, it was very cold. There was lots of snow. Long ago, travelers would cross the pass. They would have to walk. Sometimes they would get lost.

Rescue dogs were used. The dogs were big. They were strong. They had thick coats so they would not get cold. The dogs would find the people who were lost. They would drag them out of the snow. They would rescue them. The dogs were named after the pass. They were called Saint Bernards.

Find the Answers

1. Most likely, travelers don't walk across the pass now because

a. they want to get lost.

b. there are cars and trains.

c. they do not like the snow.

d. they do not want to be rescued.

2. A **pass** must be a way across a

a. lake.

b. river.

c. desert.

d. mountain.

3. Why didn't the dogs get cold?

a. They were big.

b. There were strong.

c. They had thick coats.

d. They were in the Swiss Alps.

/3

Name _____

Warm-Up 11

Wearing a Cage

A cage was made in 1856. It had steel wire hoops. Women wore the cage. They wanted to wear it. Why would women wear a cage?

At that time, women wore long dresses. The dresses were full. They spread out. Women wore petticoats to make the dresses puff out. They had to wear a lot of petticoats. The petticoats were heavy. One of the petticoats was stuffed with horsehair.

Women liked the cage. It went around their waists. It was light. It was not hot. It made their dresses puff out. The cage was called a crinoline. *Crin* means horsehair in French.

Find the Answers

1. From the story, you can tell that wearing a lot of petticoats made women

a. feel warm.

b. feel light.

c. feel French.

d. feel like a horse.

2. What was the crinoline made of?

a. horsehair

b. steel wire

c. petticoats

d. long dresses

3. Most likely, one of the petticoats was stuffed with horsehair to make the petticoat

a. itch.

b. cold.

c. stiff.

d. stink.

/3

Name _____

Why the Tree Was Scraped

Long ago, Greek girls would go to a tree. The tree was a kind of oak. The girls would scrape the tree twigs with their fingernails. Why would they scrape the twigs with their fingernails? The girls were scraping insects off the tree. The insects were very tiny. They were called *kermes*.

The girls would collect the insects. What would they do with them? They would use the insects' skin to make a dye. The dye was bright red. The girls would use the dye to **color** their dresses.

Find the Answers

1. If something is **colored**, it is

    a. used.

    b. dyed.

    c. scraped.

    d. collected.

2. What did the girls do *second* in the story?

    a. make a dye

    b. go to a tree

    c. collect the insects

    d. scrape off the insects

3. What kind of tree did the kermes live on?

    a. oak

    b. fir

    c. pine

    d. redwood

/3

Warm-Up

13

Talking with Signs

Name _____

American Indians lived on the Great Plains. There were many tribes. Each tribe had its own language. Sometimes, tribes would trade with other tribes. The tribes did not speak the same language. Still, they could talk to each other. How did they talk to each other?

People were smart. They made a clever way to talk. They used their hands to make signs. They made more than 1,000 signs. All the tribes used the same signs. They used the signs to talk.

Sign language helped traders. It also helped hunters. Hunters needed to be quiet. Using signs, they could tell each other what to do without making noise.

Find the Answers

1. What did people use to make signs?

a. feet

b. noises

c. mouths

d. hands

2. From the story, you can tell that

a. sign language has one hundred signs.

b. you do not have to make noise to talk.

c. sign language is only used by hunters.

d. American Indians did not like to trade.

3. *Clever* is to *smart* as

a. *talk* is to *help.*

b. *talk* is to *hunt.*

c. *talk* is to *speak.*

d. *talk* is to *trade.*

/3

Name _____

Warm-Up

14   Gifts for the Guests

Long ago in Egypt, a person would **host** a party. Guests would come. The host would give his guests something. It was a cone. The cone was made of animal fat. The fat was mixed with perfume.

What would the guests do with their gifts? They would put the cones on their heads. The cones would melt in the heat. The fat would run down. The guests didn't mind. They thought it was nice. They liked it because they could smell the perfume.

Find the Answers

1. From the story, you can tell that the guests thought the
   a. perfume smelled bad.   c. perfume smelled nice.
   b. perfume smelled old.   d. perfume smelled rotten.

2. When someone **hosts** a party, he or she
   a. mixes it.   c. melts it.
   b. gives it.   d. smells it.

3. What were the cones made of?
   a. animal fat   c. animal meat
   b. animal fur   d. animal teeth

/3

Name _____

Warm-Up
15   **Sodbusters**

The first settlers in Nebraska were called something. They were called sodbusters. Why were they called that?

The settlers needed to make houses. They could not make log or wood houses. There were too few trees. They made sod houses instead. Sod is a thin layer of dirt and grass. There was lots of grass in Nebraska.

The settlers busted up the sod. They cut it into blocks. They stacked up the blocks. They made walls. They even used sod on their roofs. They laid the blocks across poles.

Find the Answers

1. Where were there settlers called sodbusters?

a. Nevada   c. New Mexico

b. Nebraska   d. North Dakota

2. *Thin* is to *thick* as

a. *bust* is to *fix*.   c. *bust* is to *fall*.

b. *bust* is to *few*.   d. *bust* is to *first*.

3. Why didn't the settlers make houses out of wood?

a. There was lots of grass.   c. There were not many trees.

b. They liked to bust sod.   d. They used sod on their roofs.

/3

Name _____

Warm-Up 16

The First Rubber Ball

When was the first rubber ball made? It was made a long time ago. They were made more than 1,000 years ago. It was made by people in Central and South America.

Men would go into the jungle. They would look for a rubber tree. They would cut a slash in the tree. Sap would drip out. The sap was special. It was latex. The men would collect the latex in a cup.

Then the men would heat the latex. They would turn it into rubber. They would trade it. They would use it to make things.

Find the Answers

1. If a man coated a basket with rubber, it might be

    a. so he could eat it.

    b. so it could hold water.

    c. so he could heat it up.

    d. so he could play with it.

2. What answer is true?

    a. Trees do not have sap.

    b. No trees have latex sap.

    c. All trees have latex sap.

    d. Some trees have latex sap.

3. About how long ago did people in Central and South America first know about rubber?

    a. 10 years ago

    b. 100 years ago

    c. 1,000 years ago

    d. 10,000 years ago

/3

Warm-Up
17

Name _____

How to Be Polite in a Tepee

American Indians lived in all kinds of houses. People who lived on the grassy plains lived in tepees. People were polite. They had good manners. They did not want to be rude.

How was one polite in a tepee? A guest would bring his own bowl. He would bring his own spoon. He would eat all that he was given. It was rude not to.

How could one politely move in a tepee? One never walked between the fire and another person. That was rude. One walked behind the person. That was polite.

Find the Answers

1. The American Indians who lived in tepees lived

a. by the ocean.

b. in the woods.

c. on mountains.

d. on the plains.

2. If you were given food,

a. it was rude to eat all of it.

b. it was polite to eat all of it.

c. it was polite to eat just some of it.

d. it was rude to eat it from your own bowl.

3. *Rude* is to *polite* as

a. *good* is to *bad*.

b. *good* is to *eat*.

c. *good* is to *nice*.

d. *good* is to *walk*.

/3

Warm-Up
18

Name _____

How to Pack

Long ago, settlers went on a trail. They moved from the east to the west. They went to Oregon. They went on the Oregon Trail. The trip took many months. People rode in wagons.

People had to pack carefully. They had to bring a lot of food. They had to bring tools. They could not make the wagons too heavy. How did people pack their glass dishes? How did they pack their eggs? How did they keep the **fragile** items safe?

People packed their glass dishes and eggs in food! They put them in barrels of cornmeal! The cornmeal kept the fragile items from breaking.

Find the Answers

1. What direction did the settlers go?

   a. east to west   c. north to south

   b. west to east   d. south to north

2. Something **fragile**

   a. is very strong.   c. takes a long time.

   b. can easily break.   d. is a kind of food.

3. What might happen if the people packed too many items?

   a. The trip would take fewer months.

   b. The wagons would be too easy to pull.

   c. More people could ride in the wagons.

   d. The wagons would be too heavy to pull.

/3

Name _____

Warm-Up 19

Did Kids Drink Milk?

What did Roman children eat long ago? They ate some of the same foods we do today. They ate different foods, too. Kids drank milk, but it was not from cows. They drank milk from sheep and goats.

Kids did not eat tomatoes or potatoes. They did not eat corn. Why didn't they? Those foods grew in South America. They had not yet been brought to Rome.

A favorite Roman food long ago was dormice. Dormice are rodents. They were cooked with honey and poppy seeds. Romans sweetened their food with honey. This was because they did not have sugar yet.

Find the Answers

1. What food did *not* come from South America?

a. corn

b. tomatoes

c. potatoes

d. poppy seeds

2. Pizza is made with tomatoes. This means that children in long-ago Rome

a. ate pizza all the time.

b. could have eaten pizza.

c. could not have eaten pizza.

d. put poppy seeds on their pizza.

3. If you drink milk, it might have come from a

a. goat.

b. frog.

c. bird.

d. snake.

/3

Warm-Up 20

Fishing with Birds

People eat a lot of fish in Japan. Long ago, some fisherman used birds to catch fish. The birds were called cormorants. Cormorants are good at diving. They are good at catching fish.

The fisherman would tie a rope to his birds. He would put a ring around its neck. He would put the birds into the water. The birds would dive down. They would **snatch** up the fish.

Later, the fisherman would pull his birds back to the boat. He would take the big fish from their throats. Why didn't he take the little fish? The ring only stopped the birds from swallowing the big fish!

Find the Answers

1. The fisherman used the rope to

    a. dive down and snatch up fish.

    b. pull the birds back to the boat.

    c. take the fish from the birds' throats.

    d. keep the birds from swallowing big fish.

2. When you **snatch** something, you

    a. grab it.   c. bite it.

    b. open it.   d. shut it.

3. Where did fishermen use cormorants?

    a. India   c. Japan

    b. Niger   d. Kenya

/3

Name _____

Warm-Up 21   **Easier Not to Smile**

Today, we call photographs snapshots. We click a button. The picture is taken. It is done in a snap. It was very different long ago. The first picture was taken in the 1820s. It was not taken in a snap. It took eight hours!

It took less time by the 1830s. It still wasn't done in a snap. It took about fifteen minutes. It was hard to stay **still** for that long. People used backrests. They used neck rests. Leaning back on them helped people remain still.

People didn't smile. It was easier not to. It is hard to keep a smile for a long time. It is easier to keep your face still if you are not smiling.

Find the Answers

1. The first photograph was not of a person. Most likely, this was because a person

     a. could not stop smiling.   c. could not use a neck rest.

     b. could not click a button.   d. could not keep still for so long.

2. Another title for this story might be

     a. "Photographs Today."   c. "Who Took the First Photographs."

     b. "The First Photographs."   d. "Taking Photographs with a Click."

3. If you remain **still**, you

     a. move.   c. do not move.

     b. smile.   d. do not smile.

/3

Name _____

A High-Priced Meal

A man picked up something. He thought it was an onion.
He peeled it. He ate it. He got in big trouble! Why was
the man in trouble?

The man was in the Netherlands. It was in the 1630s.
Tulips were new to the Netherlands. Traders had brought
them. They had brought them from Turkey. Tulips grow from bulbs. The
bulbs were worth lots of money. That's because everyone wanted tulips.
People sold bulbs. People bought bulbs. The price kept going up.

What about the man who ate the onion? It was not an onion! It was a
tulip bulb! The man's meal had a very high price!

Find the Answers

1. What helped the price of tulip bulbs go up?

   a. Everyone wanted a meal.

   b. Everyone had seen them before.

   c. Everyone wanted to buy a bulb.

   d. Everyone wanted to get in trouble.

2. Where were tulip bulbs from?

   a. Turkey   c. Tunisia

   b. Norway   d. the Netherlands

3. Most likely, a tulip bulb

   a. cannot be peeled.   c. is much bigger than an onion.

   b. looks a bit like an onion.   d. does not look at all like an onion.

/3

Name _____

**Warm-Up
23**

Toothbrushes

Toothbrushes today have bristles. The bristles are made of nylon. Nylon is a kind of plastic. What did people do before plastic was invented?

Long ago, people had chew sticks. The chew sticks were twigs. The twigs came from trees. The trees had sweet-smelling wood. People would chew the twigs. They would make one end soft. They would use the chewed end to brush their teeth.

Then toothbrushes with bristles were invented. Where did the bristles come from? They came from pigs! Pigs' short, stiff, prickly hairs were used!

Find the Answers

1. A bristly hair would *not* be

a. soft.   c. short.

b. stiff.   d. prickly.

2. From the story, you can tell that

a. teeth were invented long ago.   c. people do not care about clean teeth.

b. long ago there were no trees.   d. there is more than one kind of plastic.

3. For more than one tooth, you say "teeth." What answer uses the right word?

a. If it is more than one moon, you say "meen."

b. If it is more than one boot, you say "beet."

c. If it is more than one foot, you say "feet."

d. If it is more than one spoon, you say "speen."

/3

Name _____

Warm-Up 24

A Land of Invention

We have paper. We can write on the paper. We have printing. We can print books. We have compasses. We use compasses to find north and south. We use them to find east and west. All of these things were invented in China. They were invented long ago. Other things were invented in China, too.

We eat with one invention. What could it be? It is chopsticks. One invention flies. What could it be? It is a kite. One invention was called a wooden ox. It is used to carry heavy loads. What could it be? It is a wheelbarrow.

Find the Answers

1. How many inventions were talked about in the story?

a. four   c. six

b. five   d. seven

2. What invention helps us find north and south?

a. paper   c. printing

b. a compass   d. chopsticks

3. Most likely, the wheelbarrow was called a wooden ox because

a. like an ox, it could fly.

b. like an ox, it had four legs.

c. like an ox, it was made out of paper.

d. like an ox, it was used to carry things.

/3

Warm-Up
25

Name

Why People Burned Bamboo

Long ago, people burned bamboo. They burned it in their campfires. Why did they burn bamboo? Marco Polo was an explorer long ago. He told why.

Bamboo is hollow inside. It is filled with air. When the bamboo was thrown on the fire, the air heated up. The bamboo popped open. It made a noise when it popped open. The noise was loud. It was crackly.

People burned the bamboo to make the noise. The loud, crackly noise kept them safe. It scared away wild animals!

Find the Answers

1. The hollow spaces in bamboo are filled with
   a. air.   c. fire.
   b. pop.   d. noise.

2. Most likely, the bamboo made a noise like
   a. soft humming.   c. a fly buzzing.
   b. snow falling.   d. a firecracker.

3. From the story, you can tell that Marco Polo
   a. never sat by a campfire.
   b. was not scared of wild animals.
   c. went to places where bamboo grew.
   d. did not know why people burned bamboo.

/3

Warm-Up 26

Name _____

Fuel on the Plains

Settlers went west. They went on the Oregon Trail. They went in wagons. They crossed the plains. They needed fuel for their fires. They could not burn wood. Not many trees grew on the plains. What did the settlers use?

The settlers used buffalo chips. Buffalo chips were buffalo droppings. The chips were not messy. They did not have much of a smell. They had been dried by the sun. The chips burned well. They burned with little flame. They were good for heating. They were good for cooking.

Find the Answers

1. Which way did the settlers go on the Oregon Trail?

a. east   c. north

b. west   d. south

2. Why weren't the buffalo chips messy?

a. They were good for cooking.   c. They burned with little flame.

b. They were used by settlers.   d. They had been dried by the sun.

3. Most likely, the buffalo chips the settlers used

a. were wet.   c. were old.

b. were new.   d. were fresh.

/3

Name _____

Warm-Up 27

Pitch Lake

Long ago, an explorer saw a lake. The explorer's name was Sir Walter Raleigh. It was 1595. Raleigh used the lake. He didn't use it for drinking. He used it to fix his boats. How could this be?

The lake is a pitch lake. It is in Trinidad. It is the biggest pitch lake in the world. Pitch is tar. The tar bubbles up. Its top gets hard. You can walk on the lake. You will not sink. You are not too heavy. (A car is too heavy.) Scratch off the top. Thick pitch bubbles up.

Raleigh's boat was wood. It needed to be resealed. Raleigh said the pitch was the best he had ever used to seal his boat.

Find the Answers

1. What would most likely sink in the lake?

    a. a cat   c. a mouse

    b. a kite   d. a plane

2. Most likely, if a wooden boat is *not* sealed,

    a. water will get in.   c. it will be too heavy.

    b. you can walk on it.   d. you can scratch the top off.

3. Where was the pitch lake?

    a. Turkey   c. Trinidad

    b. Tunisia   d. Tanzania

/3

Warm-Up 28

Name _____

A Secret

China

Long ago, there was a secret. The secret was kept for over 1,000 years. It was a secret in China. The secret was about silk. Silk is a type of cloth. People knew how to make silk in China.

Everyone wanted silk. It cost a lot. People paid. They paid because they did not know how to make it. Only people in China knew how.

How was silk made? It was made from worms! The worms spun cocoons. The cocoons were made of silk. Cocoon threads were woven into silk!

Find the Answers

1. Why did people pay a lot for silk?

   a. It came from China.

   b. It was made from worms.

   c. They wanted to know the secret.

   d. They did not know how to make it.

2. What was woven into silk?

   a. wood

   b. worms

   c. cocoon threads

   d. cotton threads

3. From the story, you can tell that

   a. no one wants silk cloth today.

   b. silk is no longer made in China.

   c. how to make silk is still a secret.

   d. how to make silk is no longer a secret.

/3

**Warm-Up
29**

Name _____

Pigeon Heroes

A pigeon is a bird. Some people think they are pests. Not all pigeons are pests. Some pigeons are heroes.

Long ago, we did not have the things we do today. They had not yet been invented. We did not have cell phones. Still, people needed to talk. They needed to get help. How did people ask for help? They used pigeons!

The pigeons were **trained.** They were trained to fly home. A message would be put in a can. The can was small. It was put on the bird's leg. The bird would be let go. It would fly home. People would read the message. They would send help.

Find the Answers

1. When an animal is **trained,** it is

   a. taught to do something.   c. lying on its back.

   b. sleeping.   d. taking a bath.

2. What is one thing we have today that was *not* yet invented long ago?

   a. pots   c. shoes

   b. cars   d. canoes

3. What can be said about pigeons?

   a. No pigeons are heroes.

   b. All pigeons are pests.

   c. All pigeons are heroes.

   d. Some pigeons are heroes.

/3

Warm-Up
30

Name _____

The Bad Wish

A **myth** is a story. It is a made-up tale. The Greeks lived long ago. They told a story. We still tell the tale today. The myth is about King Midas.

King Midas liked gold. He liked gold more than anything. One time, King Midas wished for gold. King Midas got his wish. Everything he touched turned to gold.

At first, King Midas was happy. Then King Midas was not happy. He found that he had made a bad wish. He could not eat. His food turned into gold. He could not drink. He could not touch people. In the end, King Midas took his wish back.

Find the Answers

1. How did King Midas feel about his wish at first?

   a. He thought it was a bad wish.

   b. He thought it was a good wish.

   c. He thought he would take it back.

   d. He thought he had not made a good wish.

2. If King Midas turned a flower to gold, he could

   a. not see it.   c. not find it.

   b. not feel it.   d. not smell it.

3. A **myth** is a

   a. tale.   c. wish.

   b. tail.   d. witch.

/3

Name _____

Warm-Up 1

Can You Run Faster Than a Flying Bird?

Can you run faster than a flying bird? Most birds fly fast. Most birds fly faster than you can run. One bird is very slow. It is called the woodcock. The woodcock is the slowest flying bird in the world.

How slow can a woodcock fly? A woodcock can fly five miles per hour. At this speed, most birds would **stall**. They would stop flying. They would drop down to the ground.

Think of a person jogging. Five miles per hour is close to the speed of a jogger. If you can run fast, you can run faster than this bird can fly!

Find the Answers

1. The story tells us

    a. what a woodcock eats.   c. how fast a woodcock runs.

    b. where a woodcock lives.   d. how slow a woodcock flies.

2. What do you know is true about a blackbird?

    a. A blackbird flies slower than a woodcock.

    b. A blackbird flies faster than a woodcock.

    c. A blackbird flies at the same speed of a jogger.

    d. A blackbird flies at the same speed as a woodcock.

3. If something **stalls**,

    a. it jogs.   c. it stops.

    b. it flies.   d. it starts.

/3

Warm-Up 2

Name _____

You and the Rhino

A rhino is a big beast. It has horns. Its horns are on its head. You are a small person. You do not have horns. Yet you and the rhino have something in common. Something is the same. What can it be?

Most animal horns are hard on the outside. They are softer on the inside. A rhino's horns are not the same as other animals' horns. A rhino's horns are hard on the outside. They are hard on the inside, too. The horns are made of keratin. Keratin is what your fingernails are made of.

If your fingernails fall off, they grow back. If a rhino's horn gets knocked off, it grows back.

Find the Answers

1. What is a rhino's horn made of?

a. bone   c. stripes

b. keratin   d. fingernails

2. How is a rhino's horn different from most animals' horns?

a. It is hard on the inside.   c. It is hard on the outside.

b. It is soft on the inside.   d. It is soft on the outside.

3. From the story, you can tell that

a. rhinos have fingernails.

b. rhinos fight with their horns.

c. rhinos use their horns to dig.

d. rhinos have had their horns knocked off.

/3

Warm-Up 3

Name _____

Seventeen Years Underground

Count to seventeen:
One, two, three, four, five,
six, seven, eight, nine, ten,
eleven, twelve, thirteen, fourteen, fifteen,
sixteen, seventeen.

1 2 3 4 5...

That is how many years one insect stays underground. The insect is a cicada. The female lays her eggs in a tree. The eggs hatch in about two months. The newborns are nymphs. The nymphs drop to the ground. They dig down. They stay underground for seventeen years! They eat plant roots.

All the nymphs come out about the same time. They finish changing into adults. The adult cicadas stay above ground. How long do they live above the ground? Do they live for seventeen years? No! They only live for a few weeks.

Find the Answers

1. How long does a cicada nymph stay underground?

    a. seventeen days   c. seventeen months

    b. seventeen weeks   d. seventeen years

2. Where does the female lay her eggs?

    a. in trees   c. on the ground

    b. in tree roots   d. under the ground

3. A fully grown cicada is

    a. an egg.   c. an adult.

    b. a nymph.   d. a newborn.

/3

Warm-Up 4

Name _____

From Ship to Building

What is a skyscraper? A skyscraper is a tall building. Where did the word come from? How did the name come about?

Ships have **masts**. The masts are large poles. Masts hold up sails. In the 18th century, a small flag was flown from the top of the ship's main mast. The flag was called a skyscraper.

People began to use the word more. They used it to describe a tall horse. They used it to describe a tall man. When the first tall buildings were built, people called them skyscrapers.

Find the Answers

1. A **mast** is a

   a. large pole.

   b. tall horse.

   c. skyscraper.

   d. small flag.

2. Another name for this story might be

   a. "Sailing Ships."

   b. "All About Buildings."

   c. "How a Name Came About."

   d. "The First Skyscraper."

3. What happened *first*?

   a. Men were called skyscrapers.

   b. Flags were called skyscrapers.

   c. Horses were called skyscrapers.

   d. Buildings were called skyscrapers.

/3

Name _____

Warm-Up
5

Don't Open the Window!

People go to a hotel. They must not open a window. Why not? The hotel is under the water! Believe it or not, there are now hotels where people can sleep under the water.

People can eat and drink. They can take baths. They can do all the things they can do in a hotel above ground. They can do even more! They can watch fish! They can watch fish outside their window, even if they wake up in the middle of the night.

Find the Answers

1. If a person stayed in a hotel under the water, he or she could

   a. take a bath.   c. open a window.

   b. walk outside.   d. lie in the sun.

2. Most likely, windows in hotels under the water

   a. open easily.   c. are always open.

   b. do not open.   d. are open in the middle of the night.

3. From the story, you can tell that

   a. the hotels under the water are free.

   b. the hotels under the water are unsafe.

   c. there were not always hotels under the water.

   d. there are more hotels under the water than above ground.

/3

Warm-Up
6

Name _____

A Fruit That Can't Go on a Train

A durian is a fruit. It grows in Southeast Asia. It is big. Some durians are as big as soccer balls. Its outside husk has thorns.

Some people like the durian. They think it tastes good. Other people do not like the fruit. Many hotels do not allow the fruit inside. It is not allowed on trains. Why is the fruit not allowed? What is wrong with it?

The durian stinks! It stinks even when the husk is still on. How bad does it smell? It smells worse than rotting fish!

Find the Answers

1. Where does the durian grow?

   a. Northwest Asia   c. Southwest Asia

   b. Northeast Asia   d. Southeast Asia

2. The outer part of the durian is the

   a. husk.   c. taste.

   b. fruit.   d. smell.

3. Why aren't durians allowed on trains?

   a. The smell makes some people sick.

   b. The smell makes some people smile.

   c. The smell makes some people hungry.

   d. The smell makes some people play soccer.

/3

Name _____

Warm-Up 7

Why People Wore Antlers on Their Eyes

The Inuit live in the far north. It is very cold in the far north. It snows a lot. Long ago, the Inuit wore antlers on their eyes. Why did they do this?

The Inuit did not want to get snow blind. Snow blindness is like getting a sunburn on your eyes. It is very painful. Until you heal, you have a hard time seeing.

The Inuit took caribou antlers. They cut long, thin slits in them. They made **grooves** for their noses. They tied the curved antlers around their heads. The Inuit could see through the slits. The thin slits kept most of the sun's dangerous rays out. With his antler goggles, the Inuit's eyes were safe.

Find the Answers

1. What animal do you know from the story lives in the far north?

   a. monkey
   b. caribou
   c. gorilla
   d. elephant

2. If a person didn't have goggles, what might he or she wear?

   a. boots
   b. pants
   c. mittens
   d. sunglasses

3. When the Inuit made a **groove** for his or her nose, it was like making

   a. a long, narrow cut.
   b. a large, white hat.
   c. a hot, tasty dinner.
   d. a soft, fluffy pillow.

/3

Name _____

Warm-Up **8**

Most Buildings Are Made Of . . . ?

What is your house made of? Is it made of wood? Is it made of stone? Most houses in the world are not made of wood or stone. They are made of mud. Mud is cheap. It is in places where there are no trees.

The largest mud building is in Mali. It can hold 3,000 people. It has thick walls. The walls have to be thick. This is so they can bear the weight of the tall, big building.

Every year, people put fresh mud on the building. How do they reach the top? They do not need ladders. They stand on wood poles. The wood poles are part of the building. They stick out of the walls.

Find the Answers

1. If the bottom of the mud building's walls were thin,

a. it could not be so tall.

b. it could be even taller.

c. it could bear more weight.

d. it could be even stronger.

2. The largest mud building can hold how many people?

a. 3

b. 30

c. 300

d. 3,000

3. Why might someone think a stone or wood house is better?

a. It is cheap.

b. It lasts longer.

c. There are lots of trees to use.

d. There are more houses made out of stone.

/3

Name _____

Warm-Up 9

Why Beekeepers Work at Night

Sometimes, beekeepers have to work at night. Why do they have to work when it is dark?

Bees live in a hive. During the day, they fly to flowers. They get pollen. They get nectar. At night, they return to the hive. Sometimes, beekeepers need to move their hives. They move them into fields that need pollinating.

The hives need to be moved at night. This is because all the bees are inside. They are not out in the fields. They cannot get lost. There is one more reason. Since bees stay in the hive at night, beekeepers are less likely to be stung!

Find the Answers

1. Bees make honey. People also use them for

   a. moving.

   b. working.

   c. stinging.

   d. pollinating.

2. Bees are more likely to leave the hive when

   a. it is light.

   b. it is dark.

   c. you are sleeping.

   d. there are no flowers.

3. If a beekeeper moves a hive after the bee has left in the morning, the bee will

   a. stop getting nectar.

   b. not sting the beekeeper.

   c. not know where to find its hive.

   d. get more nectar and pollen in the dark.

/3

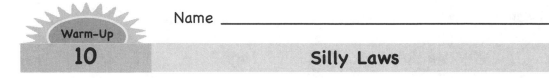

**Warm-Up
10**

Name _____

Silly Laws

Laws are passed to keep us safe. Sometimes, old laws seem very silly. They no longer make sense. For example, two old laws are about horses. What do the laws say? One says you can't pass a horse on a street. The other says horses may not be kept in bathtubs.

Other laws are about food. One says you can't slurp your soup. Another says you can't carry a hidden ice-cream cone.

One old law is about lions. What does it say about lions? It says you can't take a lion to a theater. Maybe that isn't such a silly law after all!

Find the Answers

1. How many laws are you told about in the story?

   a. two   c. seven

   b. five   d. ten

2. Most likely, the law about the lion was passed

   a. after someone tried to keep a lion in a bathtub.

   b. before someone tried to keep a lion in a bathtub.

   c. after someone tried to take a lion to the theater.

   d. before someone tried to take a lion to the theater.

3. Perhaps the law about slurping was passed because someone was

   a. passing a cook.   c. hiding in a theater.

   b. sleeping a lot.   d. making too much noise.

/3

Warm-Up 11

Name _____

A Flower That Stinks

Flowers smell. They have an **odor**. Most flowers have a nice smell. One flower does not have a nice odor. It stinks! The flower that stinks is the biggest flower in the world.

The biggest flower in the world is the rafflesia. It is also called the stinking corpse lily. How big is it? It is almost 3.3 feet across. How much does it weigh? It can weigh 24 pounds.

What does it smell like? It stinks like a dead animal. Why does it have such a bad odor? It wants flies to come. The flies pollinate the plant.

Find the Answers

1. An **odor** is

  a. a smell.   c. a weight.

  b. a plant.   d. an animal.

2. Because of its size, the rafflesia most likely grows

  a. high up on a stem.   c. far out on a branch.

  b. close to the ground.   d. on top of a leaf.

3. From the story, you can tell that

  a. no flowers smell bad.   c. some flowers smell bad.

  b. all flowers smell bad.   d. most flowers smell bad.

/3

Warm-Up
12   **Hurricane Names**

Name _____

Hurricanes are storms. The storms are big. They start over water. Hurricanes have names. Why are the storms given names? At times, there is more than one hurricane at a time. The names help people keep the storms straight.

How are the storms named? The first storm of the year always starts with an *A*. The second starts with a *B*. The third starts with a *C*. The fourth starts with a *D*, and so on. There is one name for every letter of the alphabet except for *Q*, *U*, and *Z*.

Boys and girls names are used. The names can be reused every six years. If a storm does a lot of harm, the name is never used again.

Find the Answers

1. Katrina was a big hurricane. It did a lot of harm. Most likely, the name Katrina
   a. will never be used again.
   b. will be reused next year.
   c. will be reused in six years.
   d. will be reused on a storm that does a lot of harm.

2. What name could *not* be the name of a hurricane?
   a. Ana
   b. Erin
   c. Omar
   d. Zeke

3. A big storm cannot be a hurricane
   a. if it does a lot of harm.
   b. if it does not start over water.
   c. if there is more than one at a time.
   d. if it is the second storm of the year.

/3

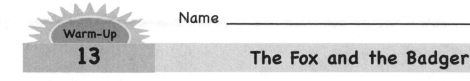

Name _____

Warm-Up
13

The Fox and the Badger

A fox follows a badger. The fox does not want to eat the badger. Why is the fox following the badger?

One of the badger's favorite foods is the earthworm. Badgers will go out at night. They will look for earthworms. They will find a good patch of earthworms. They will eat and eat.

Foxes like earthworms, too. How does a fox find a good patch of earthworms? It follows a badger! When the badger finds a good patch of earthworms, out comes the fox! The fox eats and eats.

Find the Answers

1. What happens *first*?

   a. The fox eats earthworms.   c. The fox is no longer hungry.

   b. The fox follows the badger.   d. The badger finds earthworms.

2. When does the fox follow the badger in the story?

   a. at night   c. in the morning

   b. in the rain   d. during the day

3. From the story, you can tell that a fox and a badger

   a. only eat each other.   c. always eat the same things.

   b. never eat the same things.   d. eat some of the same things.

/3

Warm-Up
14

Name _____

Tail Talking

A tiger can talk with its tail. How does a tiger say, "Hi"? How does it say, "I'm friendly"? A tiger puts its tail out. It holds the tail up high. It slowly wags it. It wags it back and forth.

How does a tiger give a warning? How does it say, "Be careful"? The tiger lowers its tail. It twitches it from side to side. The tail's message is, "I'm tense. I'm on edge. I'm stressed. Be careful. Watch your step."

How does a tiger say, "I'm excited"? The tiger's tail does more than twitch. It lashes side to side. It goes back and forth very quickly.

Find the Answers

1. How many ways are you told a tiger holds its tail in the story?

　a. one　　　　　　　　　c. three

　b. two　　　　　　　　　d. four

2. What is true about the tiger's tail when it is saying, "Hi"?

　a. It is still.　　　　　　c. It is down low.

　b. It is up high.　　　　　d. It is twitching.

3. If a tiger's tail is quickly lashing back and forth, the tiger is most likely saying,

　a. "I'm tense."　　　　　c. "I'm on edge."

　b. "Be careful."　　　　　d. "I'm excited."

/3

Name _____

Climbing a Waterfall

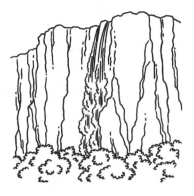

A waterfall is wet. It flows. The water drops over an edge. It goes down. You think you can't go up it, but you can! People all over the world go up waterfalls. It is a sport. How can they do this?

The people are climbers. They climb ice. They wait for winter. They wait for the water to freeze.

The climbers take axes. The axes are made for ice. They swing their axes into the ice. They put on boots. The boots have **crampons**. Crampons are steel spikes. The spikes help keep the climbers from slipping.

Find the Answers

1. What do climbers use to swing into the ice?

a. boots

b. axes

c. ropes

d. spikes

2. Why can't climbers climb waterfalls in the summer?

a. The water isn't frozen.

b. They don't use crampons.

c. Their boots will get wet.

d. They have axes made for ice.

3. Climbers use **crampons** because

a. ice flows.

b. ice is wet.

c. ice is slippery.

d. ice drops over an edge.

/3

Warm-Up
16

Name _____

The Song Most Sung

People like to sing. They sing songs. There are many different songs. What is the song most sung? How can anyone know what song it is?

It is said that one song is sung more than others. What is the song? It is "Happy Birthday to You." This song is sung all over the world. It is not always sung in English. It is sung in different languages, too.

It may be true that this song is sung more than others. Why might it be true? All over the world, people have birthdays!

Find the Answers

1. You sing a song. What do you do to a book?

   a. eat it   c. walk it

   b. read it   d. sleep on it

2. The song "Happy Birthday to You"

   a. is only sung one time.   c. is sung in different languages.

   b. is only sung in English.   d. is not sung all over the world.

3. You can only say it *may* be true that "Happy Birthday to You" is the most sung song because

   a. people do not always sing in English.

   b. people do not have birthdays all over the world.

   c. you can count every time a song is sung around the world.

   d. you cannot keep track of every song sung around the world.

/3

Warm-Up 17

Wet Money

Name _____

Get a piece of paper wet. The paper gets soggy. It falls apart. Take a piece of paper money. It could be a one-dollar bill. It could be a five-dollar bill. It could be a twenty-dollar bill. Get the bill wet. It does not fall apart! Why does the piece of paper fall apart? Why doesn't the paper money fall apart?

The piece of paper and the paper money are not made of the same thing. Paper money is not made out of paper! Dollars are made out of cloth. The cloth is made up of cotton and linen fibers. The cloth fibers last longer than paper. They are stronger. They do not break down in water.

Find the Answers

1. A cotton or linen fiber must be like a

   a. ball.

   b. penny.

   c. thread.

   d. ladder.

2. Another title for this story might be

   a. "What Money Is Made Of."

   b. "One- and Five-Dollar Bills."

   c. "Where Paper Money Is Made."

   d. "All About Cotton and Linen."

3. If paper money was made out of paper, it would

   a. not break down in water.

   b. last longer than cloth money.

   c. be stronger than cloth money.

   d. not last as long as cloth money.

/3

Warm-Up

18

Name _____

Baby Eyes That Look Big

A baby is born. The baby is small, but its eyes look very large. Its eyes look **huge** in its small head. Why do a baby's eyes look so big?

As we age, we grow. Not all of our parts grow the same amount. A baby's eyes will grow. A baby's head will grow. The baby's head will grow a lot. The baby's eyes will not grow as much as the baby's head. The baby's head will get much bigger. The baby's eyes will not look as big when they are in a much bigger face.

Find the Answers

1. A baby's eyes look big because its

a. face is big.

b. face is small.

c. face will not grow.

d. face will grow the same amount.

2. When something is **huge**, it is

a. large.

b. born.

c. small.

d. growing.

3. What do you know about the way a baby grows?

a. All body parts grow the same amount.

b. Most body parts grow the same amount.

c. Not all body parts grow the same amount.

d. Only three body parts grow the same amount.

/3

Name _____

Warm-Up
19
Charming Cobras

A cobra is in a basket. The lid is on. It is dark inside. The cobra is coiled up. A snake charmer takes the lid off. He plays music. The cobra rises up. It sticks its head up. It **weaves** back and forth.

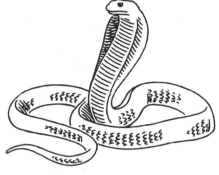

People think the cobra is charmed by the music. That is false. It is not true. It is all an act. The cobra did not rise up because of the music. It rose up because the lid came off. It rose up to scare away anything that might hurt it.

Find the Answers

1. From the story, you can tell that if there was no music,

   a. the snake would be charmed.   c. the snake would rise up anyway.

   b. the snake would not rise up.   d. the snake would stay coiled up.

2. If you are **weaving**, you are

   a. coiled up.   c. staying still.

   b. rising up.   d. moving side to side.

3. *True* is to *false* as

   a. *off* is to *on*.   c. *off* is to *weave*.

   b. *off* is to *rise*.   d. *off* is to *coiled*.

/3

Name _____

Word in Reverse

We read from left to right. We write the letters from left to right. One word is not always written this way. The letters are written in **reverse**. They are written from right to left. What is the word? Where is it written? Why is it written this way?

The word is "ambulance." An ambulance needs to go fast. It needs people to see it. It needs people to get out of its way. It has lights and sirens. The lights and sirens help people see it. It has one more thing.

It has the word "ambulance" written in reverse. The word is written on the front. Drivers can then read it the right way in their rearview mirrors.

Find the Answers

1. You can tell from the story that drivers use their rearview mirrors to

a. look under them.   c. look in front of them.

b. look behind them.   d. look to the side of them.

2. What question word is *not* answered in the story?

a. why   c. when

b. what   d. where

3. When something is **reversed**, it

a. is turned around.   c. helps people see it.

b. needs to go fast.   d. is written left to right.

/3

Warm-Up
21

Name _____

The Fishing Cat

Most cats stay away from water. They do not like to get wet. One cat likes water. It likes to get wet. It likes to swim! It is the fishing cat.

The fishing cat lives in Asia. It taps the water with its paw. Why does the cat tap the water with its paw? It is tricking fish! It taps the water like a bug. A fish comes to eat the "bug." The cat dives in! The cat eats the fish!

Find the Answers

1. Another title for this story might be
   a. "What Most Cats Eat."   c. "The Cat That Tricks Fish."
   b. "Where All Cats Live."   d. "The Bug That Taps the Water."

2. What is true about most cats?
   a. They like to swim.   c. They dive in the water.
   b. They like to get wet.   d. They stay away from water.

3. Where does the fishing cat live?
   a. Asia   c. Antarctica
   b. Africa   d. North America

/3

Warm-Up 22

Name _____

Blue from Space

You are in outer space. You look down. You take a picture of Earth. What color is planet Earth? It looks blue. Why does Earth look blue?

Earth looks blue because it is mostly water. Earth is two-thirds water. Divide Earth into three equal parts. Two of the three parts will be water. Only one part will be land.

Our planet is mostly water, but what do we call it? We call it Earth! We named it for its land. Just think if our planet was named Water!

Find the Answers

1. What word does *not* fit with the other words?

   a. land   c. lake

   b. dirt   d. earth

2. Earth looks blue from

   a. land.   c. water.

   b. space.   d. our planet.

3. Divide a pie into three equal parts. You eat one of the parts. What answer is true?

   a. You ate one-third of the pie.   c. Only one part of the pie is left.

   b. You ate two-thirds of the pie.   d. All three parts of the pie are left.

/3

Name _____

Warm-Up 23

In the Mouth of a Crocodile

People see little crocodiles in the mouths of big ones. They think the big crocodile is eating its own kind. They think it is eating its own young. Is this true?

It is not true. Crocodiles are good mothers. They do not eat their young. Mothers want to keep their babies safe. They want to help them. Mother crocodiles cannot pick up their young. They do not have arms. Instead, they open their mouths. They scoop up the little crocodiles. They keep them in their mouths. They can carry them. They can keep them **safe**.

Find the Answers

1. If a mother crocodile wants to get her babies from the nest to the water, she might

   a. eat her own young.
   b. carry them in her mouth.
   c. scoop them up in her arms.
   d. not know how to keep them safe.

2. What is the opposite of **safe**?

   a. at risk
   b. large
   c. good
   d. open

3. Most likely, if a mother crocodile has young in her mouth,

   a. she will chew.
   b. she is in the water.
   c. she is catching food.
   d. she will not swallow.

/3

Name _____

Warm-Up
24

All About Antlers

Deer have antlers. Some deer have big antlers. Some deer have little antlers. It depends on the kind of deer. Antlers are not horns. Horns stay on. Antlers fall off. Every year, a male deer grows new antlers.

Why do deer grow antlers? The antlers are like boxing gloves. Two male deer run at each other. Their antlers hit. They get locked together. The deer cannot stab each other.

Can you tell a deer's age by its antlers? No, you cannot. Old deer can have little antlers. Young deer can have big antlers. It depends on what and how much the deer eats.

Find the Answers

1. Horns are *not* the same as antlers because

   a. horns stay on.

   b. horns fall off.

   c. horns are bigger.

   d. horns are smaller.

2. Most likely, if a deer has big antlers, then

   a. it got into a fight.

   b. it did not get into a fight.

   c. it ate a lot of good food.

   d. it did not eat a lot of good food.

3. If another kind of animal goes after a deer, the male deer could use its antlers to _____ it.

   a. eat

   b. box

   c. pet

   d. stab

/3

Name _____

Warm-Up 25   **Ouch!**

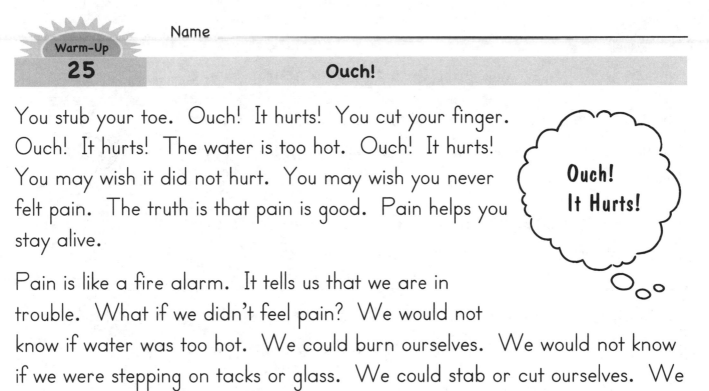

You stub your toe. Ouch! It hurts! You cut your finger. Ouch! It hurts! The water is too hot. Ouch! It hurts! You may wish it did not hurt. You may wish you never felt pain. The truth is that pain is good. Pain helps you stay alive.

Pain is like a fire alarm. It tells us that we are in trouble. What if we didn't feel pain? We would not know if water was too hot. We could burn ourselves. We would not know if we were stepping on tacks or glass. We could stab or cut ourselves. We might not even know if something was biting us!

Find the Answers

1. Pain is like a fire alarm because it

   a. burns us.   c. bites us.

   b. stabs us.   d. warns us.

2. You would most likely say "Ouch!" when you

   a. read a book.   c. bump your knee.

   b. run on grass.   d. eat your lunch.

3. What word does *not* fit with the other words?

   a. burn   c. pain

   b. help   d. hurt

/3

Warm-Up 26 — Ants for Stitching

Name _____

You get a deep cut. It needs stitches. What do you do? You use ants! You use ants to stitch up the wound! How can this be?

There are many different kinds of ants. Some ants are called soldier ants. They have very large jaws. These jaws can be used to help treat wounds. A healer is a person who helps people get healthy. In some places, a healer picks up a soldier ant. He holds its head close to the wound. The ant bites down! Its jaws clamp shut.

The healer quickly twists off the ant's head. The ant's head stays in place. It acts like a stitch. A healer will stitch up the cut with ants! Of course, in our country, you would see a doctor.

Find the Answers

1. This story is mainly about
   a. all kinds of ants.
   b. twisting off ant heads.
   c. different kinds of wounds.
   d. how one kind of ant is used.

2. *Large* is to *big* as
   a. *close* is to *stay*.
   b. *close* is to *shut*.
   c. *close* is to *twist*.
   d. *close* is to *stitch*.

3. A soldier ant is used because
   a. it has large jaws.
   b. it has small jaws.
   c. it has a large head.
   d. it has a small head.

/3

Name _____

Warm-Up 27

First in the Air

What went up in the air first? Three animals were first to go up in the air. One was a rooster. One was a duck. One was a sheep.

The year was 1783. It was September 19. It was in France. Two brothers made a balloon. The brothers filled the balloon with smoke. Now we know it is hot air that makes a balloon rise. At that time, the brothers thought it was smoke.

To make a lot of smoke, the brothers burned straw. They burned wool. They even burned old shoes! The balloon with the animals went up! It flew about eight minutes. It went about two miles.

Find the Answers

1. What date did the animals go up?
   a. November 17, 1782   c. September 17, 1782
   b. November 19, 1783   d. September 19, 1783

2. The brothers burned all but what to make smoke?
   a. wool   c. shoes
   b. rope   d. straw

3. From the story, you can tell that
   a. the smoky air was hot.
   b. the animals had all flown before.
   c. the brothers had lots of old shoes.
   d. the balloon could have flown longer.

/3

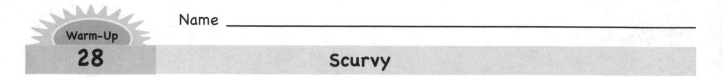

Name _____

Warm-Up 28

Scurvy

Long ago, sailors were afraid. They were afraid they would get scurvy. They would turn pale. Their gums would turn soft. Their teeth would fall out. Their cuts would not heal. The sailors did not know why they got scurvy. They did not know how to **prevent** it. Everyone was afraid of being struck down.

When did the sailors get sick? They got sick after being at sea for a long time. Today, we know why. Today, we know about vitamins.

The sailors needed vitamin C. Vitamin C is in fresh food. It is in oranges. It is in limes. It is in lemons. Sailors needed vitamin C to prevent scurvy.

Find the Answers

1. When you **prevent** something, you

   a. heal it.   c. stop it.

   b. need it.   d. know it.

2. If people want to make sure they get vitamin C, they should eat

   a. cookies.   c. crackers.

   b. oranges.   d. dried meat.

3. Most likely, the sailors got scurvy after being at sea for a long time because

   a. they had lots of fresh food.

   b. they ate foods with vitamin C.

   c. their teeth started to fall out.

   d. they had not eaten fresh food for a long time.

/3

Name _____

Warm-Up 29

What the Otter Uses

A sea otter likes to float on its back. It can eat on its back. It can sleep on its back. It can carry its young on its back. Baby otters are called pups.

Sometimes, the mother otter needs to leave her pup. She has to make sure her pup does not float away. How does the mother otter keep her pup in one place? How does she keep it from floating away?

The mother uses kelp! Kelp is a kind of seaweed. The mother wraps her pup in kelp. The kelp is anchored to the seafloor. It keeps the pup from floating away.

Find the Answers

1. The pup cannot float away because

   a. the kelp is a kind of seaweed.

   b. the pup can sleep on its back.

   c. the mother cannot leave her pup.

   d. the kelp is anchored to the seafloor.

2. The otter can do all but what on its back?

   a. eat   c. sleep

   b. run   d. carry its pup

3. *Cat* is to *kitten* as

   a. *otter* is to *pup*.   c. *otter* is to *kelp*.

   b. *otter* is to *sea*.   d. *otter* is to *float*.

/3

Warm-Up
30

Name _____

The Baby's Ride

A tornado is a wind. The wind is strong. It spins and twists. It comes down from a black cloud. It hits the ground. It spins on the ground. It moves fast and knocks things over. It lifts things up. It carries things away.

One day, a baby was sleeping. He was in his baby carriage. A tornado hit. This was in Italy. It was in 1981. The tornado picked up the baby carriage! It lifted it up! Up, up, up it went. It went fifty feet high!

It carried the carriage away. Then it set it down. It set it down over 328 feet away. Was the baby hurt? No! The baby was still sleeping!

Find the Answers

1. What is *not* true about a tornado?

   a. It twists.

   b. It moves slowly.

   c. It spins on the ground.

   d. It comes down from a cloud.

2. When was the baby picked up by the tornado?

   a. 1899

   b. 1911

   c. 2011

   d. 1981

3. How do you think people felt when they found the baby sleeping?

   a. mad

   b. sad

   c. happy

   d. sleepy

/3

Fascinating People

Name _____

Warm-Up
1

Tightrope Walker

Niagara Falls is a waterfall. It is very big. One side is in Canada. One side is in the United States. A man tried to walk across the falls on a rope. He was a tightrope walker. He called himself the Great Blondin.

The man was not afraid. His first time across, he stopped in the middle. He was high above the water. Was he going to fall? Why did he stop? The Great Blondin did not fall. He took out a bottle. He lowered the bottle with a rope. He pulled up a drink!

Twenty-one times, the man crossed the falls. Once, he rode a bicycle. Once, he pushed a wheelbarrow. One time, he carried someone on his back!

Find the Answers

1. How many times did the Great Blondin cross Niagara Falls?

   a. twenty
   b. twenty-one
   c. twenty-two
   d. twenty-three

2. If the Great Blondin started crossing the falls in Canada, he would end in

   a. Canada.
   b. Mexico.
   c. Great Britain.
   d. the United States.

3. What did the Great Blondin use to lower his bottle?

   a. a rope
   b. a drink
   c. a bicycle
   d. a wheelbarrow

/3

Warm-Up 2

Name _____

The Sailor Without Shoes

Victoria Murden was a sailor. She said, "I am going to row a boat. I am going alone. I will row across the Atlantic Ocean." No woman had ever rowed across the Atlantic Ocean before.

Murden had tried before. She had tried two times. Big storms made her stop. There were huge waves. There were strong winds. Her boat **capsized.**

Murden tried a third time. She did not take shoes. Why not? Rowing a boat is hard work. Murden needed her boat to be light. A light boat is easier to row. Murden rowed for about three months. Then on December 3, 1999, she stepped onto land. Murden had done it!

Find the Answers

1. How many times did Murden try to row across the ocean before she made it?

a. one time

b. two times

c. three times

d. four times

2. What would Murden need to take on her boat?

a. food

b. shoes

c. games

d. pillows

3. Most likely, when something **capsizes,**

a. it has shoes.

b. it tips over.

c. it is on land.

d. it is easy to row.

/3

Warm-Up

3

Name _____

What Frank Forgot

Frank Epperson was eleven years old. He forgot something. What he forgot led to a treat. What did Frank forget? What treat did it lead to?

Frank mixed a drink. He left a stirring stick in it. He forgot the drink. He left it on the porch. That night it got very cold. Frank went outside the next morning. His drink was frozen. Frank did not throw it away. He licked it. It was good. What had Frank made? Frank called it "frozen ice on a stick." It was 1905, and Frank had made the first Popsicle®!

Find the Answers

1. Where did Frank leave his drink?

    a. at school   c. on the porch

    b. in his room   d. on the table

2. What did *not* lead to Frank making a new treat?

    a. It was 1905.   c. Frank forgot his drink outside.

    b. It got very cold that night.   d. He left a stirring stick in it.

3. How old was Frank when he made the first Popsicle?

    a. five years old   c. fifteen years old

    b. eleven years old   d. nineteen years old

/3

Warm-Up
4

Name _____

Swimming Through Hot and Cold

Lynne Cox is a swimmer. She does not swim to go fast. She swims to go long distances. Lynne was going to swim across a lake. The lake is in Iceland. It is called Lake Myvatn. No one had swum across the lake before. It was too cold.

Lynne started swimming. The water was like ice. Her arms grew **numb**. Then Lynne felt hot water! As Lynne swam, she swam through cold water and then hot water.

How could the cold lake have hot parts? The inside of Earth is hot. The water was warmed by heat coming up from inside Earth.

Find the Answers

1. How many people swam across the lake before Lynne?

   a. no one

   b. two people

   c. six people

   d. ten people

2. What statement is true?

   a. Lynne swam across Earth.

   b. Lynne swam in hot water only.

   c. Lynne swam in cold water only.

   d. Lynne swam in hot and cold water.

3. If you feel **numb**, most likely, you feel

   a. hot.

   b. wet.

   c. cold.

   d. warm.

/3

Name _____

Warm-Up 5   Walking to a Lesson

Johann S. Bach was born in Germany. He was born in 1685. Bach was a **composer**. He wrote music. We still play Bach's music today.

A man played the organ. Bach wanted a lesson from the organ player. Bach said, "I will go see him. I will ask for a lesson."

The man lived far away. Bach was not rich. He could not pay for a ride. That did not stop Bach. He walked to his lesson. How far did Bach walk? He walked across Germany. He walked 250 miles!

Find the Answers

1. What does a **composer** do?

   a. cooks food   c. writes music

   b. walks fast   d. gives lessons

2. The story does *not* tell us

   a. when Bach was born.   c. how far Bach walked.

   b. where Bach was born.   d. how long it took Bach to walk.

3. In the story, Bach is

   a. rich.   c. lazy.

   b. poor.   d. cold.

/3

Name _____

Warm-Up

6   Nonstop Around the World

Jeana Yeager and Dick Rutan flew around the world. They did not stop. They did not refuel. This had never been done before. They were the first.

It took them nine days. They went in December of 1986. They had to carry all their fuel. Their cockpit was very small. This was so they could fit more fuel. Their fuel weighed almost ten times more than their plane.

It was hard to sleep and move in the small cockpit. It was only 2 feet wide. It was only 5.6 feet long. They could not stand up in it. They had to take turns flying and resting. They had to fly above and around storms.

Find the Answers

1. How many days did it take to fly nonstop around the world?

   a. six   c. eight

   b. seven   d. nine

2. At the end of the flight, the landing weight was less than the takeoff weight because

   a. so much fuel had been used.   c. they made their flight in December.

   b. their cockpit was so small.   d. they flew above and around nine storms.

3. From the story, you can tell that on other flights around the world,

   a. people flew through more storms.

   b. people stopped to get more fuel.

   c. no one tried to move in the cockpit.

   d. people did not take turns flying and resting.

/3

Warm-Up 7

Name _____

The Alaskan Flag

Alaska is a state. It has a state flag. The flag is simple. It is beautiful. Did a famous artist design the flag? No, a boy did. He was only thirteen years old. His name was Bennie Benson. He was from Alaska. He was an Aleut.

What does the Alaskan flag look like? It is blue. It has eight stars. The stars are gold. Seven of the stars make up the Big Dipper. The Big Dipper points to the last star. The last star is the North Star. The North Star stands for Alaska. Alaska is the northernmost state.

Find the Answers

1. All the other states are _____ of Alaska.

    a. east   c. north

    b. west   d. south

2. How many stars make up the Big Dipper?

    a. six   c. eight

    b. seven   d. nine

3. Most likely, the blue stands for

    a. gold, oil, and fish.   c. sky, water, and flowers.

    b. sun, rainbows, and glaciers.   d. bears, wolves, and moose.

/3

Warm-Up

8

Name _____

Gorilla Lady

Amy Vedder went to Rwanda. She went to the jungle. She went to where gorillas live. Amy wanted to learn all about gorillas. She wanted to follow them. She wanted to see how they lived.

Amy followed the gorillas. At first, the gorillas were afraid of her. They charged her. Amy learned to stay still. This is because, most times, gorillas are **bluffing**. They will run close. Then they will stop charging. They will look at you. They want to see what you do. If you stay still, they will not hurt you. They will go back to what they were doing.

Find the Answers

1. How do you think Amy felt the first time a gorilla charged her?

   a. mad

   b. lazy

   c. happy

   d. scared

2. If you are **bluffing**, you are

   a. crying.

   b. eating.

   c. fooling.

   d. jumping.

3. Gorillas live

   a. in the jungle.

   b. by the ocean.

   c. in the desert.

   d. by snow and ice.

/3

Name _____

The Mad Cook

In 1835, a cook got mad. The cook's name was George Crum. Why was the cook mad? George had sliced some potatoes. He had made French fries. A man sent the French fries back. He said they were too **thick**.

George sliced some more potatoes. He made thinner French fries. The man sent them back again! He said they were still too thick. This made George mad.

What did George do? He made French fries so thin they would break when the man tried to pick them up with a fork. Did the man send the thin French fries back? No, the man did not. He liked the new way of cooking potatoes. George had invented potato chips!

Find the Answers

1. The opposite of **thick** is
   a. new.   c. thin.
   b. mad.   d. break.

2. What happened *first* ?
   a. George got mad.   c. Potato chips were invented.
   b. French fries were invented. d. The man liked the French fries.

3. How do you think George and the man felt at the end of the story?
   a. happy   c. sleepy
   b. afraid   d. hungry

/3

Warm-Up 10

Name _____

Short Lessons

Eileen Collins went to school. She had lessons. Some lessons were very short. They were less than a minute! What type of school was Eileen in? Why were her lessons so short?

Eileen was learning how to be an astronaut. In space, she would be weightless. She had to practice eating. She had to practice drinking. She had to practice using space tools. She had to practice doing all this while weightless.

Eileen went up in a plane. The plane flew back and forth. It flew in big **arches.** At the top of each arch, Eileen felt weightless. She floated! It lasted for less than a minute.

Find the Answers

1. The story does *not* tell you that Eileen practiced

    a. biking.   c. drinking.

    b. eating.   d. using space tools.

2. What answer below has an **arch** shape?

    a. a box   c. a floor

    b. a desk   d. a rainbow

3. Another title for this story might be

    a. "Space Eating."   c. "Astronaut School."

    b. "Flying Planes."   d. "Using Tools in Space."

/3

Name _____

**Warm-Up
11**

How Gino Zoomed

Gino Tsai had a factory. It was a big factory. Gino wanted to get around his factory faster. Gino said he walked too slowly. He said his legs were too **short**. What could Gino do? How could he move faster?

Gino led a team of people. The team worked for five years. The team invented something. They invented a new kind of scooter. It was strong. It was light. It could fold up. It had a brake.

Gino zoomed around on his scooter. He went fast. People saw Gino on his scooter. They saw him zooming fast. They said, "We want one, too!" Today, the scooters are sold all around the world. They are called Razor® scooters.

Find the Answers

1. Why might Gino's scooter be easier to carry than an old scooter?
   a. It is fast and can zoom.
   b. It is light and can fold up.
   c. It is strong and has a brake.
   d. It is sold all around the world.

2. This story is mainly about
   a. a big factory.   c. a new invention.
   b. a scooter name.   d. a team of people.

3. The opposite of **short** is
   a. tall.   c. pretty.
   b. cold.   d. strong.

/3

Warm-Up 12

Name _____

From No-Good to Good

Harry Coover was a chemist. In 1942, he tried to make a plastic lens. His mixture didn't work. It was too sticky. Coover gave up. He thought his mixture wasn't any good.

Six years went by. Coover made his sticky mixture again. This time, he didn't give up on it. This time, he knew he was on to something. He knew it was something good.

What was Coover's mixture? Today, it is known as Super Glue®. Super Glue is very strong. It is used for many things. It is even used by doctors. It is used to stop bleeding. It is used to close up wounds.

Find the Answers

1. A doctor might use Super Glue to

   a. stop bleeding.   c. make a plastic lens.

   b. open up wounds.   d. make someone strong.

2. What can be learned from the story?

   a. It is good to give up.

   b. No sticky mixtures are good.

   c. Chemists do more good than doctors.

   d. Something that seems bad may be good.

3. When did Coover know that his mixture was good?

   a. 1942   c. before 1942

   b. after 1942   d. when he was six

/3

Warm-Up

13

Name _____

A Dog and Flares

Helen Thayer skied to the magnetic North Pole. She was the first woman to do this. She brought one dog. She brought flares. Why did she bring a dog and flares?

It was a very hard trip. It was filled with danger. Helen had to watch out for polar bears. Helen's dog was named Charlie. Charlie helped Helen with the polar bears. He was alert to danger. With Charlie, Helen could sleep. Charlie would wake her if a bear came near.

Helen used the flares to scare the polar bears. She would shoot the flares near the bears. The bears did not like the noise. They did not like the flame. The polar bears would leave Helen alone.

Find the Answers

1. Another title for this story might be
   a. "Walking to the Magnetic North Pole."
   b. "Helen's Trip to the Magnetic North Pole."
   c. "The Second Woman to the Magnetic North Pole."
   d. "Hunting Polar Bears at the Magnetic North Pole."

2. If you are "watchful and ready," you are
   a. alert.   c. asleep.
   b. alone.   d. afraid.

3. From the story, you can tell that Helen did not
   a. like the cold.   c. want to harm the bears.
   b. like to do hard things.   d. care if Charlie was hurt.

/3

Warm-Up

14   Name _____

Something New at the White House

Thomas Jefferson was president. He was the third president. Jefferson had something. He had two of them. He kept them at the White House. They were in cages. People wanted to see what he had. They were new to most people. Few people had seen them before. What were they?

They were grizzly bear cubs! Grizzly bears lived in the West. At that time, the United States was not as big as it is now. Jefferson bought a lot of land. He made the U.S. bigger.

Jefferson sent Lewis and Clark to explore the new land to the West. The explorers sent back plants. They sent back animals. They sent the grizzly bear cubs to the White House.

Find the Answers

1. Why hadn't people seen grizzly bears before?

  a. They were kept in cages.

  b. There were only two of them.

  c. Most people had not been to the West.

  d. Most people did not go to the White House.

2. What can you tell about the U.S. from the story?

  a. The White House is in the West.   c. Grizzly bears lived all over the U.S.

  b. It has always been the same size.   d. It has not always been the same size.

3. How many presidents were there *before* Thomas Jefferson?

  a. one   c. three

  b. two   d. four

/3

Name _____

Warm-Up
15

Dancing on Ice

Sonja Henie was an ice skater. She wanted to dance on the ice. She wanted to twirl and spin. Sonja was born in 1912. At that time, figure skaters wore long skirts. They did not dance on the ice.

Sonja's long skirt made it hard to dance. It got in the way. Sonja cut off her skirt. She cut it off above the knee. She sewed a border of fur around the bottom to keep it from flopping around.

With nothing to get in her way, Sonja danced on the ice. She twirled. She jumped high. She did nineteen kinds of spins. People liked how Sonja changed ice–skating. The judges liked it, too. The judges gave Sonja gold medals.

Find the Answers

1. How do you know people liked Sonja's new way of figure skating?

a. She jumped high.   c. She got gold medals.

b. She liked to dance.   d. She cut off her skirt.

2. From the story, you can tell that a long skirt

a. made it easy to twirl.

b. got in the way of spinning.

c. made it easy to dance on the ice.

d. did not get in the way of spinning.

3. How many kinds of spins did Sonja do?

a. twelve   c. seventeen

b. fifteen   d. nineteen

/3

Warm-Up

16

Name _____

A Lost President

Presidents live in the White House. John Adams was the second president. He was the first to live in the White House. When he went to move in, he got lost! He couldn't find his new home! How could this happen?

Today, there are paved roads. There are signs. When Adams moved in, there were woods north of the city. There were no paved roads. There were no signs. It was not clear what way his horse should go.

The White House was not all done when Adams moved in. The paint was still wet. The East Room was **bare**. There was nothing in it. The First Lady still used it. She hung her wet laundry in it!

Find the Answers

1. When something is **bare**, it is

   a. full.

   b. done.

   c. empty.

   d. painted.

2. Most likely, the first president did *not* live in the White House because

   a. he got lost.

   b. it was not done yet.

   c. there were no signs.

   d. wet laundry was hanging in it.

3. What do we have today that help us from getting lost?

   a. unpaved roads

   b. the White House

   c. horses

   d. signs

/3

Name _____

Warm-Up
17

Losing Eighty Times

Julie Krone was a jockey. She rode horses. She rode them in races. She rode them fast. Being a jockey was dangerous. You could get thrown from a horse. You could get stepped on.

One time, Julie was thrown from a horse. People did not think Julie would race again, but Julie could not stay away from the track. All she wanted to do was be a jockey.

Julie had won races before she got hurt. After she got hurt, she lost. She lost eighty races in a row! Most people would have given up. They would have quit. Julie did not quit. She began to win again. She won more than 80 races. She won over 3,500 races!

Find the Answers

1. What lesson can you learn from Julie?

   a. Never give up.   c. Stay away from danger.

   b. Quit if you lose.   d. Do what most people do.

2. *Won* is to *lost* as

   a. *quit* is to *row*.   c. *quit* is to *hurt*.

   b. *quit* is to *stay*.   d. *quit* is to *thrown*.

3. Why was it dangerous to be a jockey?

   a. You could win over 3,500 races.

   b. You could lose 80 races in a row.

   c. You could get thrown from a horse.

   d. You could stay away from the track.

/3

Warm-Up
18

Name _____

Pen Name

Mark Twain was a writer. He is **famous**. He is well known. His books are read all over the world. Twain's real name is not Mark Twain. Mark Twain is his pen name. A pen name is a fake name for a writer. Twain's real name is Samuel Clemens.

How did Clemens come up with his pen name? Clemens worked on the Mississippi River. He was a boat pilot. Pilots needed to know how deep the river was. If it was too shallow, it was not safe.

To be safe, water had to be two fathoms. Two fathoms is about twelve feet. If the water was deep enough, a man would call, "mark twain."

Find the Answers

1. *Fake* is to *real* as

    a. *name* is to *write*.

    b. *mark* is to *twain*.

    c. *boat* is to *fathom*.

    d. *deep* is to *shallow*.

2. If you are **famous**, you

    a. are a writer.

    b. are well known.

    c. have a pen name.

    d. are a boat pilot.

3. If you read a book by Spoon Fork, it

    a. could be a pen name.

    b. could not be a pen name.

    c. could not be read all over the world.

    d. could not be about the Mississippi River.

/3

Name _____

Warm-Up
19   **Why the Hedges Were Trimmed**

When Babe Didrikson Zaharias was a girl, she went to her neighbors. She asked them to do something. She said, "Please **trim** your hedges. Trim them so they are the same height."

Babe tried to make work fun. Often, she had to go to the store. She would not walk. She would run. She would run fast. Every time she would try and run faster than before.

When she ran, she would jump over her neighbor's hedges. The neighbors liked Babe. They liked how she tried to run fast. They trimmed their hedges. They trimmed them so Babe could leap over them fast.

Find the Answers

1. When something is **trimmed**, it is

   a. fun.   c. jumped over.

   b. cut back.   d. faster than before.

2. A row of shrubs or bushes that forms a fence is a

   a. hedge.   c. height.

   b. store.   d. neighbor.

3. Most likely, if Babe was told to pick up her room, she would

   a. be very mad.   c. make a game of it.

   b. ask for help.   d. say she was too busy.

/3

**Warm-Up
20**

What Ben Didn't Do

Ben Franklin was a founding father. He helped the United States become a new nation. He was an inventor. He was a writer. He did many things. There was one thing he didn't do. Ben didn't pick the **national** bird.

The national bird is a bald eagle. The bald eagle has a white head. It has a yellow beak. Ben did not want the national bird to be a bald eagle. He wanted it to be a wild turkey. He felt the wild turkey was a better bird.

Boy turkeys are called *toms*. Girl turkeys are called *hens*. Only toms can gobble. Wild turkeys eat seeds, acorns, and insects. Wild turkeys are good runners. They are good flyers, too.

Find the Answers

1. A **national** bird is one for

   a. one state.
   b. all of the nation.
   c. part of a state.
   d. part of the nation.

2. What are you told about the bald eagle but *not* the wild turkey?

   a. what it eats
   b. if it can gobble
   c. the color of its beak
   d. if it is a good runner

3. If you hear a turkey gobble, you know

   a. it is a tom.
   b. it is a hen.
   c. it is flying.
   d. it is running.

/3

Name _____

Warm-Up 21

The Old Lady That Wasn't

A lady was bent over. She looked very old. She was carrying some chickens. She saw a man looking at her. The lady dropped a chicken. She tried to catch the chicken. The chicken kept getting away. The man laughed and laughed. He thought it was funny to see the chicken get away from the old woman.

The really funny thing is that the woman was not old. She was only pretending that she could not catch the chicken. This was because she did not want the man to know who she was.

She was Harriet Tubman. She had once been a slave. She had escaped. The man had been her owner. Harriet was back to help other slaves escape.

Find the Answers

1. What was one thing Harriet did to look old?

   a. bend over   c. carry chickens

   b. stand tall   d. laugh and laugh

2. From the story, you can tell that Harriet

   a. was older than the man.   c. could have caught the chicken.

   b. wanted to be a slave again.   d. didn't care about other people.

3. If the man had known who Harriet was, he would have

   a. stopped looking at her.   c. pretended he didn't know her.

   b. made Harriet a slave again.   d. helped Harriet catch the chicken.

/3

Warm-Up 22

Name _____

Swimming at the Poles

There is a North Pole and South Pole. Only one person in the world has swum at a pole. His name was Lewis Pugh. Pugh swam at a pole on July 15, 2007. What pole did he swim at?

No one can swim at the South Pole. The South Pole is in Antarctica. Antarctica is land. It is land covered in a sheet of ice.

The North Pole is not land. It is ice over water. Most times, you cannot swim at the North Pole. It is solid ice. When Pugh swam, the ice had melted. Cracks of water showed between the ice floes. Pugh swam in the cold water. He swam over eighteen minutes wearing nothing more than a bathing suit!

Find the Answers

1. Why can't you swim at the South Pole?

a. It is on land.

b. It is too cold.

c. It is solid ice.

d. It is not melted.

2. How long did Pugh swim in the cold water?

a. less than fifteen seconds

b. exactly fifteen minutes

c. nearly eighteen seconds

d. over eighteen minutes

3. One reason no one had swum at a pole before might be that

a. the water was too warm.

b. the ice had not melted.

c. the ice floes had cracks.

d. people wanted to swim on land.

 /3

Warm-Up 23

Name _____

No One Knew

James Barry was a doctor. He was born between 1792 and 1795. He was British. He was in the army. He went to faraway places. He was a good doctor. He helped the rich and the poor. He saved many lives.

Barry died in 1865. Then people found out something. It was a secret no one had known. Barry was not a man. She was a woman!

Why did Barry dress as a man? Barry had a dream. It was to help. It was to save lives. It was to be a doctor. She lived long ago. Then, only men could be doctors. Barry made her dream come true.

Find the Answers

1. What sentence from the story does *not* tell you why Barry was a good doctor?

a. She was British.

b. She helped the poor.

c. She helped the rich.

d. She saved many lives.

2. If Barry wanted to be a doctor today, she would

a. not have a dream.

b. have to dress as a man.

c. not have to dress as a man.

d. have to be in the British army.

3. What year might Barry have been born in?

a. 1690

b. 1693

c. 1790

d. 1793

/3

Warm-Up
24

Name _____

What Saved Susan

The ice cracked! Susan Butcher and her sled fell in. She fell in the dark, icy water. No one was around. No one could help her. Susan was in Alaska. She was in a race. The race lasted many days. It was across the snow and ice.

Susan's sled was pulled by dogs. Her lead dog was named Granite. Granite took charge. He began to pull with all his might. The other dogs followed Granite. They pulled, too. Granite would not give up. He slipped on the ice, but he wouldn't stop pulling.

At last, the dogs pulled Susan and the sled out of the water. Granite had saved her! Thanks to Granite, Susan was alive and could stay in the race.

Find the Answers

1. Where was Granite?

    a. in back because he was the lead dog

    b. in front because he was the lead dog

    c. in the middle because he was the lead dog

    d. behind the sled because he was the lead dog

2. How long did the race last?

    a. many days   c. many weeks

    b. many hours   d. many months

3. What answer is *most* like Granite?

    a. will not work hard   c. will not give up easily

    b. will give up easily   d. will wait to be told what to do

/3

Name _____

Warm-Up 25

A Twisted Wire

It was morning. The year was 1903. Albert J. Parkhouse went to work.
He took off his coat. He went to hang it up. At that time, people hung
their clothes on hooks. Albert was upset. All the hooks were in use. There
was nowhere to hang his coat.

Albert picked up a piece of wire. He bent it. He twisted it. He hung his
coat on the twisted wire. Then he went to work.

Albert had done something new. He had **invented**
something! What had he invented? He had
invented the coat hanger!

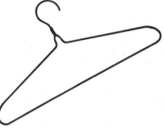

Find the Answers

1. From the story, you can tell that the first coat hanger was made from

    a. wood.   c. cloth.

    b. wire.   d. plastic.

2. Most likely, when did Albert J. Parkhouse invent the coat hanger?

    a. after he left work   c. in the middle of work

    b. before he got to work   d. soon after he got to work

3. When you **invent** something, you

    a. make something new.   c. make something tiny.

    b. make something soft.   d. make something fast.

/3

Name _____

Warm-Up

26

A Sleeping Bag with Hooks

It was time for Ellen Ochoa to sleep. Ellen did not sleep in a bed. She slept in a special kind of sleeping bag. The bag had hooks. Ellen found a place to hook her bag. Then she floated. She floated as she slept. Where was Ellen?

Ellen was in space. She was on a space shuttle. Ellen was an astronaut. Ellen drove a special type of arm. The arm was robotic. High above Earth, Ellen used the robotic arm to move supplies. She moved supplies from her ship to the Space Station.

Find the Answers

1. Ellen moved supplies from what to where?

   a. the Space Station to Earth   c. the Space Station to a space shuttle

   b. a space shuttle to Earth   d. a space shuttle to the Space Station

2. Why did Ellen have to hook her sleeping bag?

   a. so she would stay in one place

   b. so she would be high above Earth

   c. so she could use the robotic arm

   d. so she could move to the Space Station

3. What answer do you know has to be true?

   a. No arms are robotic.   c. Some arms are robotic.

   b. All arms are robotic.   d. Most arms are robotic.

/3

Warm-Up 27

Name _____

Pushing Wheels

Rick Hansen was an athlete. Then he got hurt. He was fifteen. He could no longer move his legs. He had to use a wheelchair. Rick said, "I am still an athlete."

Rick worked out. He got strong. He played sports. He raced. He played with other wheelchair athletes. Then Rick said, "I am going to take a trip."

Rick's trip took 26 months. He went through 34 countries. All that time, Rick pushed himself. He went over 25,000 miles. He pushed himself in the heat. He pushed himself in the cold. He wore out 160 wheelchair tires. He wore out 94 pairs of gloves. He never gave up.

Find the Answers

1. How many different countries did Rick visit?

a. 26   c. 34

b. 94   d. 160

2. What sentence in the story helps you know that Rick pushed himself?

a. Rick worked out.   c. He went through 34 countries.

b. He played sports.   d. He wore out 94 pairs of gloves.

3. Most likely, what would Rick tell you?

a. "Athletes never give up."

b. "Athletes must use their legs."

c. "Athletes never push themselves."

d. "Athletes cannot use wheelchairs."

/3

Warm-Up
28

Name _____

A Polite Traveler

Christina Dodwell is an explorer. She writes books. The books are about her travels. She has traveled by horse. She has traveled by dugout canoe. She has traveled by camel.

Dodwell is polite. She eats what people bring her. She says people work hard to find food. Sometimes, they look all day. It would be rude not to eat what she is given.

What has Dodwell been given to eat? She has been given strange animal parts. Sometimes, they were cold. She has been given bugs, too!

Find the Answers

1. Dodwell has traveled by all but

   a. horse.

   b. camel.

   c. crocodile.

   d. dugout canoe.

2. Most likely, some of the places Dodwell explored were

   a. not close to stores.

   b. always close to water.

   c. never close to people.

   d. always in the big city.

3. Dodwell ate bugs to be

   a. rude.

   b. silly.

   c. brave.

   d. polite.

/3

Name _____

Sixteen Sunrises

The sun rises. It rises in the morning. It is day. The sun sets. It sets in the evening. It is night. This is true for you. It was not true for Ed Lu.

Ed Lu lived in space for six months. Ed saw sixteen sunrises in one day! He saw sixteen sunsets in one day! This is because the Space Station did not stay in one place. It **orbited** Earth. It went around it. It orbited Earth every ninety minutes.

To sleep, Ed covered all the windows. He did not want the rising sun to wake him! When Ed woke up, he uncovered the windows. He wanted to see the sun rise and set all through the day.

Find the Answers

1. What would Ed have to use to know when to get up?

    a. a clock   c. a calendar

    b. daylight   d. the sun rise

2. When something goes around something, it

    a. sets.   c. orbits it.

    b. rises.   d. lives there.

3. How long was Ed in space?

    a. one month   c. sixteen months

    b. six months   d. ninety months

/3

Warm-Up

30 — Air Stunt

Name _____

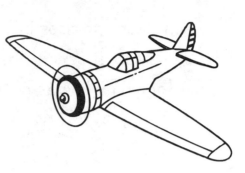

Mandy Dickenson put on a wedding dress. She got on a plane. She went high in the air. Then she jumped out. She fell through the air. She fell down toward the ground. What was going on?

Mandy was a stuntwoman. She acted in movies. She did things that were hard or dangerous. A movie had a part where someone got married in the air. Mandy played the part. She acted as if she was getting married. She did it all while she was falling!

Find the Answers

1. Most likely, what did Mandy have on over her wedding dress?

   a. a raincoat   c. a swimsuit

   b. a backpack   d. a parachute

2. Jumping over five cars on a bike would be a

   a. stunt.   c. plane.

   b. movie.   d. wedding.

3. What can you tell about Mandy from the story?

   a. She fell down a lot.

   b. She had her wedding in the air.

   c. She did not mind doing hard things.

   d. She liked doing stunts on the ground more.

/3

Answer Key

Answer Key

Interesting Places and Events

Page 9 Raining Fish
1. b
2. a
3. d

Page 10 The Black Cloud
1. c
2. d
3. a

Page 11 A City Without Cars
1. c
2. c
3. d

Page 12 Should You Wear a Raincoat?
1. b
2. a
3. c

Page 13 A Kangaroo Hero
1. d
2. b
3. a

Page 14 Nodding "No"
1. c
2. b
3. d

Page 15 The Window Washer
1. c
2. a
3. b

Page 16 Getting Ready for Antarctica
1. b
2. c
3. d

Page 17 The Only Place
1. c
2. b
3. a

Page 18 A Salt Mine
1. d
2. a
3. b

Page 19 The Biggest Antique Ever Sold
1. a
2. d
3. c

Page 20 Mail on Stilts
1. c
2. b
3. a

Page 21 Easter Island
1. d
2. c
3. a

Page 22 Getting to the Top
1. c
2. a
3. d

Page 23 A Diamond to Keep
1. a
2. d
3. c

Page 24 A Big Food Fight
1. a
2. c
3. b

Page 25 A Wet Side and a Dry Side
1. d
2. a
3. b

Page 26 The Biggest Country
1. b
2. d
3. a

Page 27 A State That Grows
1. d
2. c
3. b

Page 28 A Strange Find
1. a
2. b
3. d

Page 29 What They Race in Qatar
1. c
2. d
3. b

Page 30 Airport Island
1. c
2. a
3. d

Page 31 Too Wet for a Race
1. a
2. d
3. b

Page 32 A Name That Was a Trick
1. d
2. a
3. b

Page 33 A Bridge to Jump Off
1. c
2. b
3. d

Page 34 Idaho Before the Moon
1. b
2. d
3. a

Page 35 A Gray Suit
1. d
2. b
3. a

Page 36 A Famous Tower
1. b
2. c
3. d

Page 37 A House on Stilts
1. c
2. a
3. b

Page 38 Day and Night Are the Same
1. c
2. a
3. d

Scientifically Speaking

Page 41 The Most Bones
1. c
2. b
3. d

Answer Key (cont.)

Page 42 The Turtle's Tears
1. c
2. d
3. b

Page 43 Clam Drop
1. d
2. b
3. a

Page 44 The Longest and the Shortest Days
1. d
2. c
3. a

Page 45 The Hungry Shark
1. d
2. b
3. c

Page 46 The First Refrigerator
1. d
2. c
3. b

Page 47 A True Super Suit
1. c
2. a
3. d

Page 48 A Snake That Can Catch a Bat
1. a
2. d
3. b

Page 49 What the Owl Throws Up
1. c
2. b
3. d

Page 50 Why Astronauts Sneeze
1. b
2. a
3. d

Page 51 Popcorn
1. a
2. d
3. c

Page 52 Why Spiders Don't Get Stuck
1. a
2. d
3. c

Page 53 The Most Kinds
1. d
2. b
3. c

Page 54 The Quiet Flyer
1. c
2. d
3. b

Page 55 Different Seasons
1. c
2. b
3. d

Page 56 The Place to Throw Far
1. b
2. c
3. a

Page 57 Plant Trap
1. d
2. a
3. b

Page 58 What the Rings Tell
1. a
2. c
3. d

Page 59 Impossible to Sink
1. c
2. d
3. b

Page 60 How to Tell the Oldest Mountains
1. d
2. c
3. a

Page 61 Twinkling Stars
1. a
2. d
3. c

Page 62 Dinosaur Fossils
1. c
2. b
3. d

Page 63 Claws of the Fastest
1. a
2. d
3. b

Page 64 The Darker Hand
1. b
2. c
3. a

Page 65 Blue Blood
1. a
2. d
3. c

Page 66 Wolf Den
1. d
2. c
3. a

Page 67 Doctors Who Spread Germs
1. d
2. c
3. b

Page 68 Why We Burp
1. b
2. d
3. c

Page 69 Make It Go One Hundred Miles an Hour!
1. a
2. c
3. b

Page 70 A Horse That Bolted
1. c
2. a
3. b

From the Past

Page 73 An Old Hairstyle
1. a
2. d
3. b

Page 74 Cleaning Without Soap
1. b
2. c
3. d

Answer Key (cont.)

Page 75 A Game with a Snake
1. a
2. c
3. c

Page 76 Birthday Count
1. b
2. c
3. a

Page 77 May You Sit?
1. a
2. d
3. c

Page 78 The Moat
1. b
2. c
3. a

Page 79 The Hammock
1. d
2. b
3. a

Page 80 Left Foot, Right Foot
1. b
2. a
3. d

Page 81 How Many Knots?
1. a
2. c
3. b

Page 82 Rescue Dogs
1. b
2. d
3. c

Page 83 Wearing a Cage
1. a
2. b
3. c

Page 84 Why the Tree Was Scraped
1. b
2. d
3. a

Page 85 Talking with Signs
1. d
2. b
3. c

Page 86 Gifts for the Guests
1. c
2. b
3. a

Page 87 Sodbusters
1. b
2. a
3. c

Page 88 The First Rubber Ball
1. b
2. d
3. c

Page 89 How to Be Polite in a Tepee
1. d
2. b
3. a

Page 90 How to Pack
1. a
2. b
3. d

Page 91 Did Kids Drink Milk?
1. d
2. c
3. a

Page 92 Fishing with Birds
1. b
2. a
3. c

Page 93 Easier Not to Smile
1. d
2. b
3. c

Page 94 A High-Priced Meal
1. c
2. a
3. b

Page 95 Toothbrushes
1. a
2. d
3. c

Page 96 A Land of Invention
1. c
2. b
3. d

Page 97 Why People Burned Bamboo
1. a
2. d
3. c

Page 98 Fuel on the Plains
1. b
2. d
3. c

Page 99 Pitch Lake
1. d
2. a
3. c

Page 100 A Secret
1. d
2. c
3. d

Page 101 Pigeon Heroes
1. a
2. b
3. d

Page 102 The Bad Wish
1. b
2. d
3. a

Did You Know?

Page 105 Can You Run Faster Than a Flying Bird?
1. d
2. b
3. c

Page 106 You and the Rhino
1. b
2. a
3. d

Page 107 Seventeen Years Underground
1. d
2. a
3. c

Page 108 From Ship to Building
1. a
2. c
3. b

Answer Key (cont.)

Page 109 Don't Open the Window!
1. a
2. b
3. c

Page 110 A Fruit That Can't Go on a Train
1. d
2. a
3. a

Page 111 Why People Wore Antlers on Their Eyes
1. b
2. d
3. a

Page 112 Most Buildings Are Made Of . . .?
1. a
2. d
3. b

Page 113 Why Beekeepers Work at Night
1. d
2. a
3. c

Page 114 Silly Laws
1. b
2. c
3. d

Page 115 A Flower That Stinks
1. a
2. b
3. c

Page 116 Hurricane Names
1. a
2. d
3. b

Page 117 The Fox and the Badger
1. b
2. a
3. d

Page 118 Tail Talking
1. c
2. b
3. d

Page 119 Climbing a Waterfall
1. b
2. a
3. c

Page 120 The Song Most Sung
1. b
2. c
3. d

Page 121 Wet Money
1. c
2. a
3. d

Page 122 Baby Eyes That Look Big
1. b
2. a
3. c

Page 123 Charming Cobras
1. c
2. d
3. a

Page 124 Word in Reverse
1. b
2. c
3. a

Page 125 The Fishing Cat
1. c
2. d
3. a

Page 126 Blue from Space
1. c
2. b
3. a

Page 127 In the Mouth of a Crocodile
1. b
2. a
3. d

Page 128 All About Antlers
1. a
2. c
3. d

Page 129 Ouch!
1. d
2. c
3. b

Page 130 Ants for Stitching
1. d
2. b
3. a

Page 131 First in the Air
1. d
2. b
3. a

Page 132 Scurvy
1. c
2. b
3. d

Page 133 What the Otter Uses
1. d
2. b
3. a

Page 134 The Baby's Ride
1. b
2. d
3. c

Fascinating People

Page 137 Tightrope Walker
1. b
2. d
3. a

Page 138 The Sailor Without Shoes
1. b
2. a
3. b

Page 139 What Frank Forgot
1. c
2. a
3. b

Page 140 Swimming Through Hot and Cold
1. a
2. d
3. c

Answer Key (cont.)

Page 141 Walking to a Lesson
1. c
2. d
3. b

Page 142 Nonstop Around the World
1. d
2. a
3. b

Page 143 The Alaskan Flag
1. d
2. b
3. c

Page 144 Gorilla Lady
1. d
2. c
3. a

Page 145 The Mad Cook
1. c
2. b
3. a

Page 146 Short Lessons
1. a
2. d
3. c

Page 147 How Gino Zoomed
1. b
2. c
3. a

Page 148 From No-Good to Good
1. a
2. d
3. b

Page 149 A Dog and Flares
1. b
2. a
3. c

Page 150 Something New at the White House
1. c
2. d
3. b

Page 151 Dancing on Ice
1. c
2. b
3. d

Page 152 A Lost President
1. c
2. b
3. d

Page 153 Losing Eighty Times
1. a
2. b
3. c

Page 154 Pen Name
1. d
2. b
3. a

Page 155 Why the Hedges Were Trimmed
1. b
2. a
3. c

Page 156 What Ben Didn't Do
1. b
2. c
3. a

Page 157 The Old Lady That Wasn't
1. a
2. c
3. b

Page 158 Swimming at the Poles
1. a
2. d
3. b

Page 159 No One Knew
1. a
2. c
3. d

Page 160 What Saved Susan
1. b
2. a
3. c

Page 161 A Twisted Wire
1. b
2. d
3. a

Page 162 A Sleeping Bag with Hooks
1. d
2. a
3. c

Page 163 Pushing Wheels
1. c
2. d
3. a

Page 164 A Polite Traveler
1. c
2. a
3. d

Page 165 Sixteen Sunrises
1. a
2. c
3. b

Page 166 Air Stunt
1. d
2. a
3. c

Leveling Chart

Page #	Flesch-Kincaid Grade Level	Page #	Flesch-Kincaid Grade Level	Page #	Flesch-Kincaid Grade Level
Interesting Places and Events		**Scientifically Speaking** *(cont.)*		**Did You Know?** *(cont.)*	
9	0.7	62	1.8	116	0.8
10	0.9	63	0.0	117	1.5
11	1.2	64	0.0	118	0.7
12	1.9	65	0.5	119	0.7
13	1.9	66	1.3	120	1.2
14	0.1	67	1.4	121	1.7
15	0.9	68	0.1	122	1.7
16	0.9	69	0.5	123	0.7
17	1.9	70	1.6	124	1.4
18	0.7	**From the Past**		125	0.0
19	1.6	73	0.6	126	1.0
20	0.6	74	1.1	127	1.5
21	1.8	75	1.1	128	1.1
22	1.5	76	0.4	129	0.0
23	1.8	77	1.0	130	0.2
24	2.0	78	1.3	131	1.3
25	0.5	79	1.7	132	1.6
26	1.9	80	0.5	133	1.3
27	1.9	81	1.0	134	1.7
28	1.8	82	0.0	**Fascinating People**	
29	2.0	83	1.5	137	1.6
30	1.6	84	0.9	138	1.9
31	1.7	85	1.5	139	0.9
32	1.7	86	0.2	140	0.7
33	1.7	87	1.3	141	1.6
34	1.7	88	1.1	142	1.3
35	0.6	89	1.9	143	1.3
36	1.6	90	1.8	144	1.6
37	0.8	91	1.9	145	0.9
38	0.5	92	1.7	146	1.6
Scientifically Speaking		93	1.8	147	1.9
41	1.7	94	1.7	148	1.8
42	0.8	95	1.6	149	1.1
43	0.0	96	1.4	150	1.9
44	1.9	97	1.8	151	1.7
45	0.9	98	0.7	152	0.1
46	1.9	99	0.7	153	1.5
47	0.6	100	1.9	154	1.5
48	0.5	101	0.8	155	1.1
49	0.5	102	0.8	156	2.0
50	1.6	**Did You Know?**		157	2.0
51	1.8	105	0.4	158	1.7
52	1.5	106	1.8	159	1.5
53	1.8	107	1.9	160	1.1
54	1.4	108	1.4	161	1.2
55	0.6	109	1.9	162	1.7
56	0.7	110	1.4	163	1.6
57	1.1	111	1.9	164	2.0
58	0.7	112	0.3	165	1.4
59	1.5	113	1.6	166	1.3
60	1.3	114	1.8		
61	1.2	115	1.4		

Tracking Sheet

Interesting Places and Events		Scientifically Speaking		From the Past		Did You Know?		Fascinating People	
Page 9		Page 41		Page 73		Page 105		Page 137	
Page 10		Page 42		Page 74		Page 106		Page 138	
Page 11		Page 43		Page 75		Page 107		Page 139	
Page 12		Page 44		Page 76		Page 108		Page 140	
Page 13		Page 45		Page 77		Page 109		Page 141	
Page 14		Page 46		Page 78		Page 110		Page 142	
Page 15		Page 47		Page 79		Page 111		Page 143	
Page 16		Page 48		Page 80		Page 112		Page 144	
Page 17		Page 49		Page 81		Page 113		Page 145	
Page 18		Page 50		Page 82		Page 114		Page 146	
Page 19		Page 51		Page 83		Page 115		Page 147	
Page 20		Page 52		Page 84		Page 116		Page 148	
Page 21		Page 53		Page 85		Page 117		Page 149	
Page 22		Page 54		Page 86		Page 118		Page 150	
Page 23		Page 55		Page 87		Page 119		Page 151	
Page 24		Page 56		Page 88		Page 120		Page 152	
Page 25		Page 57		Page 89		Page 121		Page 153	
Page 26		Page 58		Page 90		Page 122		Page 154	
Page 27		Page 59		Page 91		Page 123		Page 155	
Page 28		Page 60		Page 92		Page 124		Page 156	
Page 29		Page 61		Page 93		Page 125		Page 157	
Page 30		Page 62		Page 94		Page 126		Page 158	
Page 31		Page 63		Page 95		Page 127		Page 159	
Page 32		Page 64		Page 96		Page 128		Page 160	
Page 33		Page 65		Page 97		Page 129		Page 161	
Page 34		Page 66		Page 98		Page 130		Page 162	
Page 35		Page 67		Page 99		Page 131		Page 163	
Page 36		Page 68		Page 100		Page 132		Page 164	
Page 37		Page 69		Page 101		Page 133		Page 165	
Page 38		Page 70		Page 102		Page 134		Page 166	

Congratulations

to

_____

for completing

_____

_____

_____
Signature

_____
Date